FACILITY MANAGEMENT

INDIAN & GLOBAL BEST PRACTICES

Dr. Adv. Harshul Savla

Ar. Pallavi Patil

INDIA · SINGAPORE · MALAYSIA

Notion Press Media Pvt Ltd

No. 50, Chettiyar Agaram Main Road,
Vanagaram, Chennai, Tamil Nadu – 600 095

First Published by Notion Press 2021
Copyright © Dr. Adv. Harshul Savla, Ar. Pallavi Patil 2021
All Rights Reserved.

ISBN 978-1-68563-305-9

TESTIMONIALS

"I have known Dr. Harshul as a through Real Estate Professional who is very well versed about the Sector, I'm sure his experiences will help one and all"

SBI's First Woman Chairperson, Arundhati Bhattacharya

"Congratulations! Dr. Harshul for your amazing endeavor of creating one of India's most comprehensive literature on the Real Estate Sector. It is an excellent series of books and great learning for those who have it. I know that you will soon have a much larger audience for your work"

National President NAREDCO, Dr. Niranjan Hiranandani

"This is one of the most comprehensive set of Real Estate Literature, I strongly recommend to all"

President Elect CREDAI National, Boman Irani (Rustomjee)

"Adv. Harshul Savla is a budding and promising Entrepreneur in Real Estate Industry in MMR region with keen insight and grasp of Strategy, Numbers and Statistics. He is a great addition to the Managing Committee Team of CREDAI MCHI"

President CREDAI MCHI, Deepak Goradia (Dosti Realty)

"Harshul is known to me for a decade, he is an astute Advocate and a celebrated Author. His understanding of Real Estate and its nuances is exhaustive. His work will be a reference guide / point for the new entrants in the sector"

President NAREDCO Maharashtra, Ashok Mohanani (Ekta World)

"Real Estate is a very vast subject. There are very few who understand the theoretical and practical nuances of Real Estate Sector, I am glad to note that you have studied the same in great depth and your analysis will be very helpful to the industry."

Chief Engineer (Development Plan) MCGM, Shri V.P. Chithore

"Adv. Harshul Savla has a very good exposure and knowledge of the Real Estate Sector. He has excellent vocabulary skills and speaks with confidence and clarity on matters of Real Estate. I feel his commitment of sharing knowledge inspires many young Real Estate professionals and he is truly focused on bringing a positive impact in the industry in times to come"

President PEATA India, Ar. Samir Hingoo

"Harshul was part of my team, assisting me in executing my responsibilities as a core team member of JLL India. He has a deep understanding of the Real Estate market, trends and policies"

CEO India & MD Market Developments Asia – Colliers, Ramesh Nair

"Well Researched, I wish this Book all the Success!"

President Bombay Management Association & Director JBIMS, Dr. Kavita Laghate

"Harshul Savla presents a perfect blend of academia and practical hands-on experience. I am proud to see him excel in all fields"

Former Director JBIMS, Dr. Chandrahauns Chavan

"Dr. Harshul is an avid researcher on the subject of Real Estate. I am sure readers will find his work of immense value to them"

Head Department of Law – University of Mumbai, Dr. Rajeshri Varhadi

"Advocate Harshul is a thoughtful researcher and a prolific writer, his ability to make most complex subject; simple and lucid is remarkable. He is extremely insightful on the subject matter of Real Estate. I'm sure he will produce a good read"

CEO Haj Committee of India & Former Registrar University of Mumbai, Dr. M.A. Khan

"I have mentored Harshul's Ph.D. thesis and I am extremely proud of his Research Skills"

Head of Research Department, Sydenham Institute of Management Studies, Dr. R.K. Srivastava

"This book is a must read for all; I personally endorse Dr. Harshul's Research"

CEO Wockhardt Foundation & Executive Director Wockhardt Ltd., Sir Dr. Huzaifa Khorakiwala

"I am sure Dr. Harshul's books will be an ideal start for anyone wanting to understand about Real Estate Sector in India"

COO – P.D. Hinduja Hospital & Medical Research Centre, Joy Chakraborty

"Harshul has a perfect understanding of issues being faced by the Built Environment. He is an excellent Research person, a good mentor for young talent and we are proud to have him on our panel of Guest Faculty at RICS SBE"

Associate Dean & Director – RICS School Built Environment, Amity University Mumbai, Amol Shimpi

"Harshul is one of the young and upcoming participants of today's real estate industry and I'm sure he will go on to shape and influence it in future"

Director Kanakia Group, Ashish Kanakia

"I wish Dr. Harshul's initiative on contributing content around Real Estate in India via this book all the success!"

Director – Asia Pacific Capital Markets, JLL, Priyank Shah

ABOUT THE AUTHOR

Dr. Adv. Harshul Savla (MRICS)

Dr. Adv. Harshul Savla (MRICS) is a Principal Partner of M Realty (Suvidha Lifespaces) which has successfully completed more than 1.2 million sq.ft. in last 30 years across Mumbai City under the able leadership of Mr. Pramesh Rambhiya. CRISIL India recognized Dr. Harshul as "Young Thought Leader" and Realty NXT featured him as "Young Turk of Real Estate Sector". He has won the prestigious CREDAI-MCHI Golden Pillar Award in the category of Best Debutant Real Estate Developer and has been awarded "Young Achiever of the Year" by ET NOW, CNN News 18, ZEE Business, MAHARASHTRA Times, ABP News, MID DAY and Realty Quarter.

Dr. Harshul has worked as EA to Ramesh Nair, Former CEO and Country Head at JLL, India and has worked in the Wealth Management Team at TATA Capital where he was awarded the National Award for Exemplary Performance. He is a perfect blend of Corporate Experience along with stellar education credentials of Ph.D., LL.M, LL.B, MBA and BMS.

Dr. Harshul is a World Record Holder for the Record of "Maximum Degree from Single University" and his World Record is mentioned in World Book of Records London, The British World Records, International Book of Records, International Talent Book of Records, Exclusive World Record, Asian World Records, Global Records & Research Foundation, Amazing Indian Records, World Records India, India Book of Records, Kohinoor Vidyasamrat, Champion Book of World Record, High Range Book of World Records etc.

Dr. Harshul was awarded Doctorate (Ph.D.) for his Thesis on REITs (Real Estate Investment Trusts) which is first such thesis in India on the said subject and the Thesis is also available in the form of a book. Apart from this he is an NSE Certified Market Professional - Level 4 and has done a course on 'Strategic Real Estate Management' from ISB, Hyderabad.

Dr. Harshul is "Co-Chairman: Statistics & Standards" at CREDAI National, which has more than 13,000 Real Estate Developers as its Members and has presence in 217 Cities (21 State Chapters). As a matter of fact, he is one of the youngest Office Bearer in the Managing Committee of CREDAI-MCHI wherein he is the Convener of Research & Analytics Wing and looks into the Learning and Development Initiatives of CREDAI MCHI. Dr. Harshul is also the National Head of the Committee on E-Learning and Masterclass at CREDAI National.

Dr. Harshul is also an Amazon Best Selling Author and has authored more than 15 books on the Real Estate Sector, making his books one of India's most comprehensive literature on Real Estate Sector. Some of his books are: ERA Post RERA, Real Estate Laws, Reality of Realty, Real Estate Valuation, Affordable Housing, NBFC & HFC Crisis, Fractional Ownership & REITs, Insolvency & Bankruptcy Code, Self-Redevelopment & Reviving Stalled Projects, Digitalizing

Real Estate Sector in Built Environment, Building Information Modeling, Green Buildings, Facility Management etc. He regularly writes articles for fortnightly business magazine "Property House" and may other newspapers and journals.

Dr. Harshul is also a Visiting Faculty at the prestigious RICS School of Built Environment, Mumbai Campus. He teaches the subject 'Real Estate Development Process' to Management Students at the Mumbai Campus. He is also Guest Lecturer at REMI - The Real Estate Management Institute, Mumbai. He was Invited to conduct Session on REITs in India for Developers Members of NAREDCO and was one of the youngest Member Developer to do so. He has also delivered a lecture at PEATA (I) on Future of Realty. He is also a renowned moderator for panels discussing various aspects of Realty and has moderated more then 20 panel discussions so far. Recently, Dr. Harshul was acknowledged by Business World and Realty Plus "40 under 40" list as Real Estate's Young Turk 2021

CO-AUTHOR

Ar. Pallavi Patil DACA C-DAC, DMK, MBA (Marketing), ADDM

Ar. Pallavi Patil is a Founder of New Startup "The Digital Pod" A 360 Marketing Company (2021) & Also Former Founder of Established Studio MaxVision(2004) which was Specialized in Real Estate Marketing into Architectural Hyper-realistic renderings for Eminent Architects like Deepak Mehta Architects, Reza Kabul Architects & Prestigious Developers like Progressive Developers, Shah-Chedda Architects, Supreme Parivar, Ekta Developers, Shreepati Group of Companies which has completed more than 3000+ renderings in last 20 years across India & Abroad Almost 500 + Developers & 200 + Architects, She has vast experience in the field of Façade Design, Real Estate Marketing, Brand Management, Marketing Collaterals, Outdoor Advertisement, Video Marketing , Virtual Reality, 360 Interactive Media, & Corporate Presentation for Residential, Commercial, IT Parks, Education, Hotels & Entertainment Centre's

Project portfolio across Mumbai, Navi Mumbai, , Lonavala, Karjat, Pune, Hyderabad, Chennai, Bangalore, Noida.

Ar. Pallavi Patil DACA C-DAC, DMK, MBA (Marketing), has completed Bachelor of Architecture from Mumbai University (2001) from Dr.D.Y. Patil College of Architecture Mumbai with First Class (Honors). She has completed a Diploma in Advanced Graphics Arts from National Multimedia Resource Centre from C-DAC Pune(2002). Done Masters in Marketing Management (2015-18) from Prestigious B-school Welingkar's College of Management Studies Mumbai. She Has also Specialized in Advanced Digital Marketing with Google Certifications.

Ar. Pallavi Patil was a Full-time Faculty at the prestigious RICS School of Built Environment, Mumbai Campus. She is a Versatile Teacher teaching the specialized subject like Advanced Marketing management, Customer Relationship Management, Marketing & Sales Management, Introduction to Architecture & Building construction, Urban Planning & Governance, Sustainability in Property Development, Main Elective Subjects like Marketing Communications & CRM, Digital Technologies & Social Media Marketing with 3 Years of Fulltime Experience for BBA, MBA Real Estate & Urban infrastructure & Construction Project Management Programs.

She Has Conducted ELP Training at RICS for Real Estate Laws & Sustainability for Facility Management. Has Taken Session in different Architectural colleges for Career Pathways after Architecture & Green Buildings & Technologies in Civil Engineering Colleges.

Her Research Interest Include 360 Marketing Strategies for Real estate, Brand Management, Customer Relationship Management, Marketing Strategies for Real estate, Sustainability for Real estate,

Digital Technologies & Social Media Marketing. Completed research on "TO STUDY MEANS OF MARKETING COMMUNICATION STRATEGIES USED BY REAL ESTATE DEVELOPERS IN INDIA DURING THE COVID 19 PANDEMIC" published in International Journal of Research in Humanities, Arts. (2020)

RESEARCH TEAM

Ankit Dey

MBA – CPM (RICS SBE, Amity University, Noida)

B-Tech – Civil Engineering (B. S. Abdhur Rahman Crescent Institute of Science and Technology)

Atharva Zaparde

BBA – REUI (RICS, SBE Amity University, Mumbai)

Deepak Kumar

MBA – CPM (RICS SBE, Amity University, Noida)

BE – Civil Engineering (Bannari Amman Institute of Technology, Tamil Nādu)

Ebey Simon Abraham

MBA – REUI (RICS, SBE Amity University, Mumbai)

B Tech – Electrical and Electronics Engineering (Kerala Technological University)

Gazal Joggy

MBA – CPM (RICS, SBE Amity University, Mumbai)

B. Tech – Civil Engineering (MG University)

Ignatius Victor

BBA – REUI (RICS, SBE Amity University, Mumbai)

Nithin Ramachandran

MBA – CPM (RICS SBE, Amity University, Mumbai)

PGDM – Advanced Construction Management (IIIC)

BTech – Civil Engineering (MG University)

Shubham Dilip Konde

MBA – REUI (RICS SBE, Amity University, Mumbai)

B. Arch (Savitribai Phule Pune University)

Syed Junaid Hashmi

MBA – CPM (RICS SBE, Amity University, Noida)

B. Tech – Mechanical Engineering Amity university

CONTENTS

TABLE OF FIGURES

1. INTRODUCTION AND OVERVIEW-FACILITIES MANAGEMENT

1.1   FM DEFINITION

Management is the knowledge and experience of delivering and attaining assigned goals using available resources such as labour, material, and machines, as well as monitoring them to ensure that they are done in the best and most cost-effective manner possible.

Buildings, shopping malls, townships, offices, commercial complexes, hotels, schools, industries, and industrial complexes are all examples of the built environment.

- **The Facilities refers to the infrastructure including amenities at any property or built environment.** Thus, the management of facilities of any built environment is termed Facility Management. All the infrastructures need manpower, material & other resources to maintain & operate them for the ease of users & in cost-effective planning.

- **Facility Management acts as the function to achieve it.** Facility management ensures that the proper process is followed at the right time and that the right skill sets and knowledge are used to complete and deliver the given work.

As a result, it helps to reduce or eliminate the chance of redo work, delayed responses or completion of work, accidents, complaints, cost increases, and decreases in productivity. Infrastructure operational life cycle cost and manpower operational difficulties.

1.2   FM EVOLUTION

BEGINNING

The objective of the observer mainly influences the Facility Management definition. Even though the definition of Facility Management changes with objective, the mission and vision are the same. Within the **last 40 – 50 years the Facility Management industry has escalated.** This advancement is mainly due to the changes occurring in the demographics and demography within the surroundings. From the 1980's the concept of Facility Management started gaining its grip in the construction industry.

Due to this very reason, many professional institutions were built up for Facility Management and the importance has gained enough popularity.

Some suggest that the Facility Management establishment had taken place along with the American Railroad in the 1800s. To date, there is no definite proof of the introduction of the term "Facility Management", but the literature reviews indicate that the term had emerged within the construction sector in the 1800s in America. Facilities Management made its way to Europe from the United States in the mid-1980s. From 1986 to 1992, it swiftly grew across Europe after its initial introduction in the UK in the mid-80s. Understanding the beginning of the Facility Management must be given priority as it clarifies the need for Facility Management in the industry.

SIGNIFICANT IMPACT OF CULTURAL DIFFERENCES

Through the various studies by researchers, it was identified how countries with diverse economic milestones impart Facility Management in their geography.

- The Multiple Levels of Facility Management are considered by the type of culture the country possesses.

- Therefore, the facility Management differs from region to region.

- As time progress it is a common practice by an organization to pass over the development stages and directly proceed to the corporate resource.

Comparing the cultural differences between the USA and UK helps to study how different is the Facility Management from region to region.

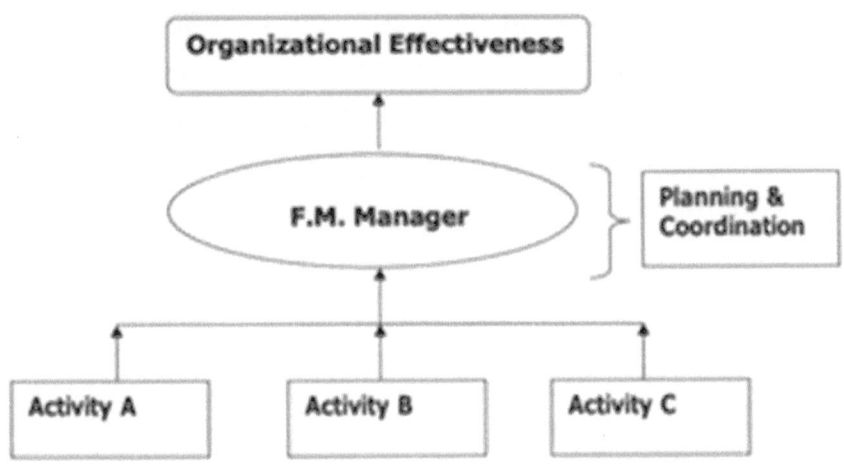

Figure 1.1 American Style for Facilities Management.

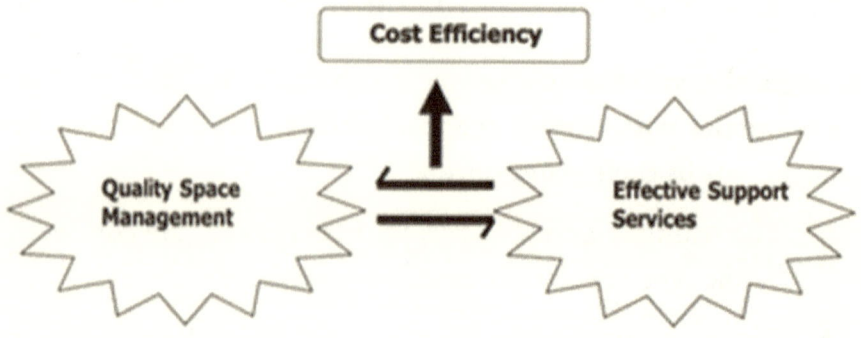

Figure 1.2 British Style for Facilities Management

The pictures show how different the two styles are concerning proposal and performance. The US Facility Management technique was more process and result oriented as it is cantered on planning and synchronizing the activities involved. The benefit is that comprehensive work processes exist for keeping track of and inspecting purposes, but the disadvantage is that this method is not human-cantered and can be regarded as a non-socially obligated paradigm. In the British technique, Facility Management is centred on the environment and service quality which is extremely broad in the emotion that it is more receptive to one's definition. while also implying less reliance on predetermined work routines. Feelings and emotions of the stakeholders are taken for this style of management.

PRACTICES FOLLOWED

- **Facility Management is all about management.** The general practice is a managerial method, not a technical method. The realization that resources may be managed for productivity launched the management's history as a unique social function many years ago.

- **Facilities management is a relatively young field** with which some individuals may be unfamiliar. Facilities Management is in charge of a property's planning, development, maintenance, and operations.

- **A diversified mix of office buildings has accumulated over perhaps fifteen years.** Designers, office managers, property managers, and building services managers are all examples of people that work in the construction industry.

- **Managers of institutional services, consultants in all of the aforementioned fields,** and commercial consultants. Various service suppliers and 'in-house' donors have discovered few commonalities shared foundation in claiming membership in FM.

- **FM has lasted nearly 40 years as a management discourse,** with one international professional body committed to its duplication and a variety of national institutions on several continents, yet it is still going firm.

- **FM's scope has now expanded far beyond real estate management** and the inheritance of property upkeep. Facilities are now seen as well thought out company assets.

1.3 FM SERVICES

Facility Management enables each facility to offer and operate with a high level of responsiveness, accuracy, and consistency. Facilities management oversees ensuring that all services are in sync with one another. The Facility Manager oversees everything.to keep the facilities up to date and cost-effective.

Facility Management encompasses a wide range of services that support the customer's or property's core business.FM Services have been divided into two categories: soft services and hard services, according to some. Some of them have Technical and Non-Technical Services that are separated into two categories. The classification of FM services is depending on the type of property or the industry It could be a township, a commercial complex, or something else.

Corporate offices, shopping mall, office, residence, or event. FM services are provided regularly under an annual contract or on a one-time basis for a limited time, such as public events, deep cleaning, or on-call services.

Any Professional or Total Facility Management firm can provide an FM Solution & Services package that includes all FM Services as well as new modules. As market demand and consumer demand dictate, more and more FM services may be provided. Services/modules for FM are the following are listed:

- Facility Management Core Services
    - **Security**
    - **Housekeeping**
    - **Engineering / Technical Services**
    - **Utility Management**
    - **AMC / Warranty Management**
    - **Landscape Maintenance**
    - **Asset Management**
    - **FM Stores Management**
    - **Pest Control Services**
- Facility Management Consultancy & Project Consultancy
- FM Help Desk
- Inspection / Audits (Fire, Safety, Energy, PDI & PPI, FM Audit, Infra Audit)

- Customer Care Management
- Pre-Possession Deep Cleaning (PPDC)
- Event & Event Facility Management
- Club / Guest House Management
- Lift Style Consultancy & Interiors
- Deep Cleaning / Total Cleaning Solutions
- Payroll & Office Support Services
- Property Management (incl. Rental Help Desk)
- Vendor Management / Procurement Services
- Transport Management (Educational Institutes & Industries only)
- InfoTech Facility Management (Hardware & Software)
- Health, Safety & Environment Module
- Infra Solutions
- Solar: Solution, O & M, and Consultancy
- Other Associated Services (Mail Management etc.)
- F&B / Canteen O&M
- Manpower / Labour Supply

Facility Management Services -Scope of Work

Facility Management Core Services

1. **Security Services:** The hiring/employing party's assets, which include persons and property (movable/non-movable), are protected by security services, which are engaged on a contract or a rolling basis.

Dangers by implementing well-defined preventative actions, which are accomplished through keeping a high level of awareness by acting as a deterrent to illegal and inappropriate behavior steps taken in response to any indications of criminal activity, emergencies, such as a fire, and then taking steps to limit the damage and reporting such incidences to the employer/customer, police, and emergency services.

Facility Management (FM) Services' Security Services Management & Operational Administration module is critical.

The fundamental goal of a security service is to protect the customer's or employer's people, property, and assets. Security Manpower, often known as personnel, is uniformed, and professionally trained for the job. Security services are important not only for protection but also for the customer/employer of the built environment or facility's operational management and profitability. It is necessary for a greater understanding to take place. Due to various current security requirements or locations, it is necessary to specify the Facility.

Security services in information technology might be network security services or data security services. Security Services, on the other hand, are methodical in FM strategy to managing and protecting people, property, and assets following customer requirements/requirements of the employer.

Security services can be performed in-house or outsourced to a third-party security firm or a facilities management firm. For achieving performance and quality, choosing the correct Security Services is critical. Before you hire or contract a security guard, make sure you do your research. Service providers must conduct thorough research and inspections of their services, their business operations.

House Keeping Services: It is described as providing services for the cleaning of the built environment under Facility Management. It refers to the operation and management of daily/ planned cleaning activities and tasks for any property or location. Housekeeping is a term used in FM to describe the cleaning and upkeep of a property or institution. Cleanliness, orderliness, and general property/facility care are also included in the definition of housekeeping.

For any building or facility, housekeeping services are a must. It comprised both manual and automated housekeeping. The scope of "House Keeping" will include people and materials for any property's shared areas.

The Following Are the Responsibilities of Housekeeping:

- Sweeping the entire common area on all floors at the specified intervals. This does not, however, include sweeping and cleaning within tenants' homes, such as in townships.

- Cleaning of the community bins that have been erected in the common area.

- All common areas need to be cleaned.

- Furniture in common lobby spaces should be cleaned or wiped down.

- Cleaning of common area doors/windows/ventilators, if applicable.

- Cleaning and scrubbing of stairwells and railings daily.

- Security cabins, security guard shelters/huts, and watchtowers are cleaned and mopped.

- Lifts are cleaned and mopped daily.

- Cleaning Venetian blinds and curtains in the common area (if any).

- Dusting of equipment, attachments, and fixtures in the common area according to the schedule.

- Cleaning/washing of communal toilets twice a day (Floor & wall dado), disinfectant installation.

- Cobwebs must be removed (As & when required)

- Cleaning of the buildings daily.

- Any other service task that may develop because of unforeseen circumstances, with mutual consent.

- The "House Keeping Service" must be performed every day of the month (excluding national holidays and specified festival holidays).

2. **Engineering / Technical Services: Operations, Preventive Maintenance, and Corrective Maintenance are some of the activities involved.** The FM Company will oversee maintaining and operating the systems and services that have been installed in the property or facility. Electrical, mechanical, and civil engineering services were limited to maintenance and operations.

   The following are the operational and maintenance activities that any FM company must perform:

   - Electrical System Operation & Maintenance (O&M) includes electrical substations, panels, street lighting, common area lights in lobbies, post-top lanterns, and garden lights, among other things.

   - Basic troubleshooting and power restoration in the event of a property network failure.

- O&M of the entire property for electrical upkeep in the shared areas

- Liaison with Electricity Company

- Property Plumbing Network Operation and Maintenance (O&M).

- O&M of pumps & water valves

- Attending to pipe leakages in the common area

- Attending to the overflow from building tanks

3. **Utility Management: The FM Company manages and coordinates a variety of utility services, including the following:**

- Water extraction by a pumping system that has been established.

- Water distribution to residential buildings

- Reading, billing, and collection of water meters (if meters installed)

- Testing for water quality (on extra charges basis)

- Dealing with contaminated water

- Ensure the generators are ready to provide power backup installed in the township for public use.

- The availability of diesel for the functioning of the diesel generator set.

- Making payments to local statutory authorities and service providers for common area utility bills, such as electricity and water.

- Communication with the Pollution Control Board.

- If water tankers are required to meet water supply needs.

4. **AMC/ Warranty Management: The Annual Maintenance Contract (AMC)/Warranty**

Administration solution is a collaborative service that provides visibility and management of AMCs/Warranties and their associated assets for all types of organizations' property's infrastructure equipment, plants, and machinery. The client will undergo AMC with FM COMPANY or directly with the equipment manufacturer/service agency for the varied FM Company proposes the following option for Annual Maintenance Contract: Machines and equipment that have been installed. The cost of AMC, as well as parts and spares. The Client is responsible for supplies, labor, and other costs.

For Any Choice, the FM Company will supply the following services:

- Administrative and renewal functions for AMCs.

- Contract information is available right away.

- Keep track of all maintenance contracts that have been purchased by the company. Information about the consumer and the assets they own.

- Customer notification about expiring maintenance contracts.

- Keep track of the equipment that is being supported or serviced by agencies or manufacturers.

- Ensuring that maintenance services are completed on time.

- Preventive maintenance programs that are flexible and detailed to ensure maximum equipment availability under contract

- Notify/update customers about expected increases in AMC service calls. (If there are any)

- Assist in the completion of a preventative maintenance task by facilitating and tracking the skill set, components, and tools required.

- The FM Company will be solely responsible for organizing maintenance and operating all the property's systems and services. If maintenance services are contracted out to FM, The FM Company will oversee selecting and evaluating candidates. collaborating with such an organization.

- The client is responsible for all costs associated with the repair, replacement, unintentional damage, high consumable usage, or labour that are not covered by the module.

- 12.In general, the following items/machines are included in the Warranty Management/AMC:

- Lifts / Escalators

- Sewage Treatment Plant (STP)

- Water Treatment Plant (WTP)

- DG Sets

- CCTV

- Electrical Substation & Associated Equipments.

- Fire Fighting & Fire Alarm System

- Over Head & Under Ground Water Tanks Hygiene Cleaning

- Parking Systems

- Access Control System

- Any other equipment/systems installed at the property/ facility.

5. Garden / Landscape Maintenance Services:

This refers to the upkeep of any property's green spaces, such as gardens, lawns, planters, and inside planters.

The Following Activities will be included in the Scope of Work:

- Ongoing maintenance of parks and gardens.

- When necessary, remove vegetative growth.

- Get rid of the weeds.

- Lawn and grass trimming and cutting

- Plant, tree, and shrub pruning according to need and timetable.

- Bushes and hedges hedging

- Watering lawns and plants as needed daily.

- The Gardeners will do maintenance tasks as needed.

- Soil tilling (Gudas) at regular intervals.

- Use of insecticides and fertilizers as a preventative measure (Urea).

- Termite treatment for grass (if necessary) is not included in the price. Scope of work and will be charged additional depending on the treatment.

- Grass / liquid manure treatment for complete grass area (after grass termite treatment) to boost grass greenery is not included in the scope of service and will be charged separately as per treatment.

- Other than regular pesticide spraying as a preventative measure, any treatment for Plants will be charged extra depending on the disease, and charges will be adjusted accordingly, separately informed.

- Garden and other planted areas cleaning and maintenance

- 15.Manure and disinfection are two of the most important aspects of the job.

- Upkeep of potted plants in the communal area/garden.

- Watering of green spaces daily.

- 18.Landscaping planning and consultancy activities are not included in the project. Contract said

- Technical Team – A horticulturist and a lawn expert will oversee the project.

- At the site, one visit per month is allowed.

- Any other service work that may arise as a result of a contingency agreed upon by both parties.

- The "Garden Maintenance Services" must be performed every month (excluding national holidays and selected festival holidays).

- For any garden maintenance utility expenditures (electricity and water), The client is responsible for the services.

- Land excavation, plantation, new plant costs, and periodic landfill costs/charges, among other things, are not included. If necessary, the same will be done at an additional cost based on current market prices, with expenses to be borne by the customer.

- Adequate store/office space with basic facilities would be supplied on-site for the above-mentioned services.

6. **FM Help Desk:** This is a cutting-edge facility management module that was developed in the year 2008. The FM Help Desk

serves as a communication hub for occupants, end-users, vendors/ contractors, and customers of any facility. A building or a facility.

The following duties will be handled by the

Help Desk:

- Occupants will be provided a dedicated helpdesk number to use as a single point of contact for all FM queries, complaints, and ideas.

- Liaison with the Client's representative daily.

- Maintaining a close eye on FM activity.

- Management and coordination of FM services daily.

- Management of occupant complaints.

- Keeping track of complaints and requests

- Complaints are resolved

- Printing and delivery of bills

- 9.Billing and collection

- 10.Customer Relationship Management

- Collecting feedback

- Survey of satisfaction and expectations

- Customer performance reporting

- Keep in touch with the occupants.

7. **Value-Added Services:** The services supplied by an FM corporation to individuals for a specific need or requirement are known as value-added services (VAS). It could happen only once or frequently. VAS has a wide range of applications based on the needs of the individual.

8. **Pest Control:** Facility Management Services also includes pest control. Regularly, it includes the following activities:

- The use of an approved pesticide for general pest management by the government regularly. In the common area, the company has appointed professionals.

- Control of vectors.

- Inspection and treatment of breeding sites.

- Operation Fogging (on periodic intervals)

- Beehives are removed. (As and when needed)

- Disinfectants are used in bin areas and other areas as needed.

- Material, labor, and equipment rental costs are not included.

- Any additional specialist pest control services, such as termite treatment and wood-destroying insects. Borer control, rodent control, and so on.

The Facility Management Services depicted above are basic/core facility management services that are required, if not required, for any built environment or property. Depending on the situation, a variety of services may be added to the Facility Management Services. the customer's requirements the list of additional services was previously mentioned. During the development or building of the property, facility management services are also necessary. During the development phase of the property, services such as security and housekeeping are required. Any facility management organization should have integrated facility management solutions at this time.

In Today's Market, a single point of contact for all facilities management services is required.

The ability to integrate Facility Services is critical to success and customer satisfaction.

2. STRATEGIC ROLE OF FACILITY MANAGEMENT

2.1   INTRODUCTION

(Boden, 2014) All organizations are affected by strategy, which influences everything from how and what raw materials are acquired, to how consumers are given access to resources and assistance. To define the meaning of strategy, (Abdul et al., 2012) Strategy is a technique of thinking about how to keep track of your strengths and weaknesses to maintain your business's development and success.

Learning, finding, and creating are all aspects of strategy that support an organization's best practices to gain a competitive benefit. It is very crucial in a present world where the demand for the facility management industry is soaring day by day.

2.2   IMPORTANCE OF STRATEGIES

- **To make effective decisions, you will need a strategy.** You will also need to update your best practices, which will affect quality, time, and cost.

- **It is a method for assisting managers in making long-term business choices,** as well as handling activities and best practices that contribute to the success of businesses and organizations.

- **FM is a vital profession that not only focuses on economic skills** but also recognizes the value of social and environmental advantages. Targeting FM at a strategic level is based on leadership excellence that leads to a strategic route, while effective learning and innovation assist to bring value to the FM organization.

- **In any organization, strategies have a vital part in determining profit margins**, customer happiness, and the recognition of the FM organization. Furthermore, this will give good delivery on quality, pricing, and time that meets the needs of the consumers, as well as raise customer expectations for products and services.

- **Align real estate (space) and facility operations** in a way accelerating business goals, capability, and performance of the organization.

(Boden, 2014) There are a variety of difficulties to moving strategic partnerships ahead, and these barriers might hinder a company's potential to gain a competitive edge. Some of the major barriers include:

- **Long-standing concerns** have been raised regarding a proclivity for risk aversion and a reluctance to engage with the private sector during the pre-procurement stage. By not connecting with the market before procurement, commissioners are missing out on crucial information. Speaking with providers from many industries and investigating how services are offered in other areas might reveal unique and innovative solutions.

- **Financial restrictions** have generated concerns about the reduction of high-quality (and well-paid) commissioning and contract management employees.

- **An Issue in contract management**: Instead of measuring the success of the facilities management team through the core business output, financial performance and cost reduction are the most often cited performance indicators and more than half of facilities functional groups are either part of a shared services infrastructure organization or report to a head of CRE or the CFO.

2.3 PROCESS

(Reeve, 2001) It is a 4-step activity that involves knowing scenarios, facilities, circumstances, and wants, assessing the adjustments necessary, and implementing an authorized plan.

UNDERSTANDING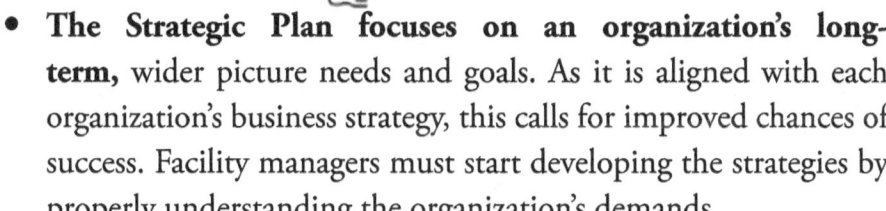

- **The Strategic Plan focuses on an organization's long-term,** wider picture needs and goals. As it is aligned with each organization's business strategy, this calls for improved chances of success. Facility managers must start developing the strategies by properly understanding the organization's demands.

- **The Task that a Strategic Facility Plan team** does is reliant on the organization's unique wants and must cover both long-range and strategic planning, based on existing internal analyses and business imperatives. It should, on the other hand, cover the evaluation of existing facilities as well as the conception, design, and execution of new ones.

- **To Effectively assess the demands and compare present conditions to those needs,** a detailed grasp of the current situation is required.

- **Strategic Plans often include a mix and range of suggestions aimed at maximizing the value of a company's assets.** The facilities manager considers the organization's purpose, vision, culture, and fundamental values, as well as the company's present position and real estate asset base, as well as the company's general direction and ongoing initiatives, how the business could develop, and how such changes might influence the company's real estate demands.

- **Following a thorough understanding of these factors,** a strategy that is driven by business is used to assess the facility of organizations and create concrete targets.

- **The Strategic Facility Plan squad and manager investigate** the different company targets of each business unit and include these targets into the plan of facility analysis to produce a complete plan.

- **This Specifies space in future and real estate requirements** depending on company objectives, beginning with projected services, anticipated workforce changes, and possibly fresh technology.

- **These criteria are used by the team to forecast upcoming usage,** needs, and operational expenses. The second stage will begin once a clear knowledge of the Strategic Facility Plan aims, also the approval procedure and success have been achieved.

ANALYSIS

The FM Manager and the team begin to explore how to aid present facility demands with continuing **expectations and challenges** after a precise characterization of the business's condition has been created. Workforce, industrial operations, culture and structure of the organization, requirements by government regulatory are examples of these expectations and challenges. **The Gap that the SFP will fill is determined by comparing existing inventory and circumstances to projected demands.**

To Evaluate and fill this Gap, as well as the options and suggestions produced, several tools can be utilized.

- **Scenario Planning:** Planning tools that aid in predicting the changes that may affect your company. Also, it could be educational simulations of various operational circumstances. This approach might be used with other models to guarantee that planners engage in strategic thoughts. This process may be very effective for recognizing strategic challenges and objectives.

- **Systematic Layout Planning:** Mouther created the SLP technique to build conceptual block layouts. The technique integrates complicated data categories one at a time until a block pattern is created, making it a strategic to the tactical tool.

- **Brainstorming:** This method assures that diverse points of view and perspectives are represented, especially if the people are well-chosen. On the negative side, too much input may result in discrepancies. When done correctly, brainstorming may lead to unique, original ideas that might otherwise go unnoticed.

- **Benchmarking:** Benchmarking is for comparing and evaluating your company against others, wherever in the globe, to learn about ideas, methods, and measurements aiding in the performance of the organization. It also involves the fact to accept that others are better at something while also being intelligent to learn from them too.

- **Organizational simulation**: In organizational studies and strategic management, this is a popular approach. This tool is designed to help you learn how businesses work. The organizational simulation may be used to represent a system for managing facilities depending on a thorough understanding and analysis of the influence of connected facility options and activities.

PLANNING

Major Steps while Planning includes writing out the key areas to be tackled, assess locations, zoning, costs, labour, competition, and any other important success elements, analyse the risks involved, develop suggestions, develop a marketing campaign to win management support; and obtain financing and finally get approval and begin the next phase.

ACTION

- **The SFP is now available for execution after it has been approved.** The creation of a particular initiative or project to supply additional, changed, or modified space to suit the organizational requirement is generally required for the implementation of an SFP. In some cases, contract organizations may oversee some projects, particularly big new space programmers.

- **Facilities must be active as core team members in these situations to guarantee that the stages of the project are integrated.** Irrespective of the methods used to create an SFP, it should be seen as a live document that presents results and offers thoughtful suggestions for implementing the plan within a reasonable period while being flexible enough to adjust as business demands.

- **Flexibility to adjust to changing situations may be necessary while implementation is underway** because of any substantial change in market circumstances, economic outlook, or other causes.

- **Facility management strategies are a significant facility management tool** used to assist the company, and they must constantly be aligned with the organization's objectives in order to be successful.

2.4 CONCLUSION

Changes in organizational culture and practices will have a significant impact on how the Strategic Facility Plan is implemented. Various types of business including those for financial gains and also non-profit, and government bodies, will have differences and similarities in business units, business boom or loss, and other factors.

This Study divides Companies into three categories: service businesses, manufacturing businesses, and governmental/ academic institutions. Within each category, there are considerable similarities and preferences.

Service Firm

- A continuous focus on people and facilities design in a service firm is evident most of the time.

- The majority of these companies have centralized data collection and systems in place, as well as defined data-use procedures. Service firms have similar approaches to defining and achieving business and facility goals, as well as generally short planning timeframes.

Manufacturing Firm

- Because each Location supports distinct equipment, employees, and produced goods, SFPs in manufacturing firms are generally done on a location basis than company-wide.

- In addition, several companies in this category employ decentralized data collection and interpretation, and usage strategies.

Government Institution

- Variation in politics, financial budgets, expected public sentiment, and service levels are all factors that affect government and academic institutions.

- Long-term planning is the standard for companies in this domain since they use both centralized and dispersed information collection.

"Due to the considerable difference in these different types of sectors, the projected SFP will need to be changed to some amount to account for the above-mentioned issues impacting the planning horizons of these different types of companies. As a result, identifying the sorts of organizations is the first step in establishing this personalized SFP."

3. BUILDING EFFICIENCY THROUGH FACILITIES MANAGEMENT

3.1   INTRODUCTION

Energy demand grows in line with the global population growth, and carbon dioxide emissions rise well. Buildings spend around **40% of the energy they consume** during their lifespan, with heating and cooling accounting for **60-70 percent** of it. Constructing buildings with minimal energy needs that do not affect the environment is the most appropriate approach. Design engineers can make a significant contribution towards energy conservation, decrease emissions, and most importantly, significantly cut heating and cooling expenses within the structure. (Potkany, Vetrakova and Babiakova, 2015). Businesses squander roughly **30% of the energy consumed in their commercial buildings, according to the EPA,** while buildings account for **32% of global energy usage and 19% of energy-related greenhouse emissions.** Companies are turning to facilities managers to give advice and guidance on how to enhance the energy efficiency of their buildings as they become more focused on methods to decrease energy waste. Facilities management is well positioned to utilize local operational efficiency efforts to detect and act to increase the efficiency of energy usage throughout their facilities since they are responsible for maintaining the functionality, comfort, and safety of the physical environment. Facility managers have a better grasp of the site's unique problems and possibilities, and can advise on how to effectively combine humans, process, and technologies to achieve maximum efficiency. (@ *Www.Environmentalleader.Com*)

3.2   WHAT IS EFFICIENCY

(Lemaire, 2008) By efficiency of a building, it mainly focuses on the energy consumption of a building and its services. Lesser and wise consumption makes a building more energy efficient. The efficiency of a facility refers to how closely its energy consumption every square meter of floor area corresponds to recognized energy consumption standards for that kind of structure under certain climatic circumstances.

3.3   TOOLS AND TECHNIQUES FOR ACHIEVING BUILDING EFFICIENCY

(Lemaire, 2008) Building energy efficiency techniques are methods for reducing a building's energy usage while simultaneously improving its level of comfort. These can be subdivided into:-

- **Lowering the Demand for Heating**

  Keeping the building's surface area to a minimum:- The amount of space open to the outside through external walls and ceilings is determined by the form of the structure. Keep this exposed space to a bare minimum to save power. A simple square or rectangle floor design is the most cost-effective to build and heat. When a home has a complicated form, it increases the exposed area and also the energy and construction expenses.

- **Increasing the structure's fabric's insulation:-** Conduction accounts for the remaining two-thirds of heat loss through bases, flooring, sidewalls, ceiling, roofing, windows, and doorways. High levels of insulation in the attic, sides, foundations, and doorways can limit heat transfer in and out of the structure due to conduction. The U-value of windows should be as low as possible.

- **Choosing an appropriate heating system:-** The most apt and effective method of heating for a building will differ depending on the structure's intended purpose. Radiant heating may be an effective type of heating for buildings that are used only occasionally (such as churches) or have huge air volumes (such as industrial units). Traditional centralized hot water systems will be more successful in buildings that are utilized more frequently and have lower air volumes. Modular boilers should be utilized for non-domestic structures with variable loads to avoid heaters operating at higher loads. Because of its greater season efficiency, condensing boilers is used instead of traditional boilers; when properly operated, they may be up to 30 percent more efficient than regular boilers. The installation of climate adjustment devices and under-floor heaters where condensing boilers are installed will increase their efficiency by lowering water flow temperature.

1. **Lowering the Demand for Cooling**

    - **Keeping excess glazing to a minimum:-** Windows must be positioned to give enough day lighting while minimizing solar gain. Large expanses of glass will enhance solar heat intake in the summer and heat loss in the winter, making it more difficult to maintain a suitable indoor climate.

    - **Shading:-** Exterior shade, mid-pane blinds and internal blinds can all help to minimize solar gains.

Interior blinds are the least efficient way of reducing solar gains since the heat has already entered the area. Exterior blinds are the most effective, but they can be hard to maintain and regulate for glare control. Mid-pane blinds are frequently used as a compromise. When glare and solar gains are not a problem, they can be elevated, and when they are, they may be lowered. Solar gains to the east and west are much more difficult to regulate and will need the use of movable shading devices.

- **Glass with solar control:-** Glazing comes with a variety of selective coatings that change the characteristics of the glass; the best glazing has the maximum light transmission and the smallest solar heat gain factor. This will allow for more daylight while lowering solar gains. All major glass producers, including those with coatings like those mentioned here, give statistics on the characteristics of their products.

- **Equipment with a lower heat output should be chosen:-** Choosing office equipment with a lower heat generation and assuring that equipment has appropriate controls that automatically turn it off when not in use will help minimize cooling demands. Flat-screen monitors may considerably minimize heat gain while also lowering equipment energy use and maximizing workplace space utilization. These advantages generally outweigh the increased price of flat screen displays.

2. Lowering the Amount of Energy Needed in Ventilation

- **Design of Building:** Cross ventilation, in which air may move from one side of a building to the other, is the most effective kind of natural ventilation. Buildings must be no more than 12-15 meters deep in order for this to operate successfully. Natural ventilation may be performed in deeper plan areas by incorporating central atria and utilizing the "stack effect" to draw air from the outside perimeter and up into the center of the structure.

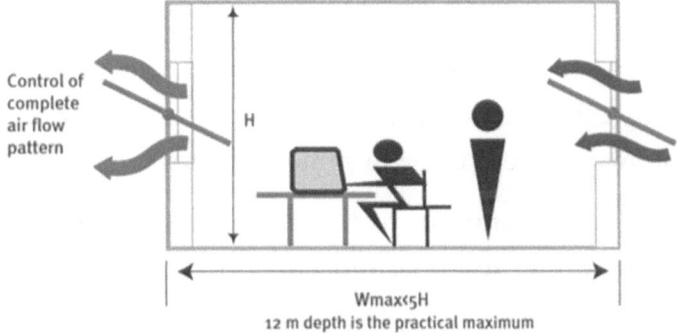

Figure 3.1   Cross Ventilation

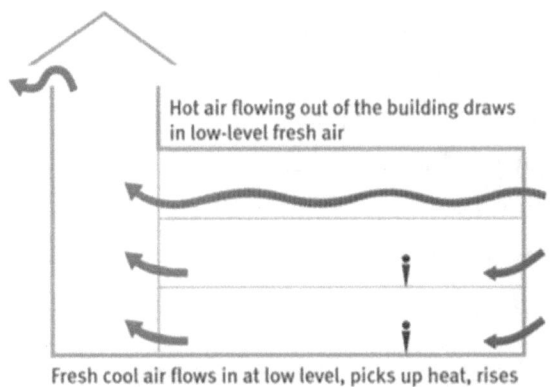

Figure 3.2   Stack Ventilation

Appropriate Design of Window:

- **Building occupants should have easy control over windows,** as well as regulated ventilation that does not blow papers off tables or generate draughts. In the summer, night ventilation can be an efficient way to keep the temperature comfortable.

- **Because it seems illogical to open windows before leaving a building at night,** it is critical that building occupants understand how the facility is meant to be run or that appropriate control mechanisms be included if night ventilation is utilized.

- **Maintaining security and managing wind and rain** are other important considerations. High ambient noise levels or air pollution may prevent usage in some instances.

  1. **Reducing the amount of time that office equipment and appliances are used:** In order to operate, most companies rely on a variety of office equipment. it is commonly acknowledged that these things have become vital to daily operation. Office equipment is the quickest energy consumer in the corporate sector, accounting for 15% of total office power usage. By 2020, this is anticipated to increase to 30%. There are other related expenditures that are sometimes neglected, such as increased cooling requirements to offset the excess heat produced by this equipment. Because ventilation and air conditioners cost a lot of energy, it makes excellent financial sense to utilize them only when strictly necessary.

  2. **Human ideas and good housekeeping**

     - **Developing an Energy Policy:** Energy saving commitment must start from the top and be accompanied with a tailored mission statement and energy strategy. It's also crucial to identify an energy champion. This may be the owner or manager in very small firms, but in bigger organizations, a designated staff person will frequently enhance engagement and awareness throughout the whole organisation. Develop a procurement policy that requires energy-efficient items to be mentioned when purchasing to demonstrate commitment of management.

- **Involving Employees:** Because all employees have a role in energy conservation, employees must be informed of waste areas and properly educated to operate equipment and controls. Motivate employees by soliciting feedback and encouraging them to examine their own working methods in order to save energy. Those that utilize the equipment on a regular basis typically have the greatest suggestions. Competitions, campaigns, and group initiatives are all excellent methods to get support. Emphasize the advantages of enhancing the working environment and offer employees a sense of responsibility over energy conservation.

- **Scheduling walk-arounds:** Regularly conducting excellent housekeeping walk-arounds in your facility to determine where energy is being used. Keep track of when equipment is utilized and take any necessary waste or repair actions. Because energy consumption patterns change throughout the day, it's a good idea to do a number of walk-rounds at different times to figure out where and when energy is being wasted. Walking through your workplace after everyone else has left, before someone comes in, during the day and when offices are vacant provides you an indication of what equipment is left on outside of business hours.

- **Take readings from the meters:-** Meter readings might provide insight into the office's energy consumption. During and after office hours, meter readings can be utilized to assess electricity usage. These data show how much energy is consumed every hour that the office is empty, and how much energy is consumed while no one is in the building. In most offices, night-time energy use should account for a tiny portion of energy demand.

3.4 HOW FACILITIES MANAGEMENT TEAM AND FM MANAGERS BECOME A TOOL

Businesses squander roughly 30% of the energy consumed in their commercial buildings, according to the EPA, while buildings account for **32% of global energy** usage and **19% of energy-related greenhouse emissions**. Companies are turning to facilities managers to give advice and guidance on how to enhance the energy efficiency of their buildings as they become more focused on methods to decrease energy waste. **Facilities management is well positioned to** utilize local operational efficiency efforts to detect and act to increase the efficiency of energy usage throughout their facilities since they are responsible for maintaining the functionality, comfort, and safety of the physical environment. **Facility managers have a better grasp of the site's unique problems and possibilities, and can advise on how to effectively combine humans, process, and technologies to achieve maximum efficiency.**

There are three methods facility managers may enhance the efficiency of their building systems, whether it is as part of a company's corporate sustainability program, an operational investment plan, or just to save money on utilities.

Ensure that energy-consuming equipment is managed in a proactive manner.

The key to ensuring that buildings systems remain functional, comfortable, safe, and efficient is to guarantee that machinery is well-taken care and managed through periodic inspections and preventative maintenance. Because attention is typically focused on more important concerns, equipment check-ups are sometimes ignored. When maintenance is neglected for an extended length of time, it can lead to decreased equipment efficiency or asset damage. Maintenance work of energy-consuming equipment should be done on a regular basis to discover leaks, repairs, and replacements. Operation and maintenance, agreements, routine maintenance, and compliance scheduled preventive maintenance work may all be tracked using a CMMS system, especially if you have a big portfolio of locations. The information gathered by this sort of technology provides insight into asset performance and may be utilized to increase energy efficiency even more.

Use HVAC Controls and Lightings to their Full Potential.

- **Facilities managers** can save energy by improving the performance of lighting and HVAC systems with the help of control solutions.

- **Lighting that remains** on in empty spaces or rooms that are completely illuminated by daylighting wastes energy, regardless of technology.

- **Occupancy sensors** are one of the most prevalent forms of lighting controls, which switch lighting on instantly when motion is detected and off if the area is left.

- **Sensors can be mounted on the wall,** in the ceiling, in the corner, or on the unit itself. Automatic daylighting systems may read external lighting conditions and raise or reduce illumination level to maintain a basic level of illumination in places where enough light source is available.

- **Timers are another technique to ensure that lighting in big**, open spaces is switched off when it isn't needed. A basic timeclock or software controls can be used to do this. Lighting can also benefit from lighting control systems. Photocells and motion sensors may be added to most car park pole lights and wall-packs.

- **The key to getting the most out of lighting controls** is to double-check that the coding is right, and that the system is working correctly on a regular basis.

- **When developing, deploying, and managing these control systems,** it is also vital to keep health and human comfort in mind. In a similar way to lighting controls, sensor-based HVAC control and smart switches can be employed.

- **To control room temperature, facilities managers** can replace old mechanical thermostats with programmable ones. Backlit and a display unit, a 7-day programmable clock, remote temperature monitoring, are all features to look for.

- **Facilities Managers** should obtain corporate direction on setback levels if programmable thermostats are being deployed as part of a broader upgrade effort; requirements may vary for various seasons and geographic locations.

- **Ensure that programmable thermostats** are configured to maximize process and boost comfort conditions once they have been installed.

- **The time clock is one element of these** machines that is sometimes neglected. Because setback temperatures are based on hours of the day, facility managers should verify that all thermostats are configured with the right time of day.

Updating of Current Building Systems

- **There is a lot of potential in upgrading older, existent buildings to make them more efficient by changing the building systems.** When firms restrict the scope of their refit to a few widely understood measures and push out a green technology investment package throughout their business, the retrofit approach will be most effective. While identifying and piloting solutions on a facility basis is possible, larger adoption of "one-touch" retrofit initiatives is more cost-effective and beneficial.

- **Facilities managers are frequently requested to participate at various phases of the retrofit process,** involving onsite audits to identify retrofit possibilities, coordinating with procuring on technology standards and specifications, retrofit itself, monitoring, and service. Consultants can be hired to assist businesses with the retrofitting process. They may offer advice on which retrofit bundles are the most cost-effective, as well as assist with financing.

- **GameStop, for example, collaborated with a consultant** to make educated judgments regarding the timing and extent of lighting and HVAC system retrofits. According to reports, their refit effort has resulted in a **30 percent drop in total energy use.** These measures have helped GameStop reduce its environmental footprint and increase operational efficiency. Replacing of windows and doors, as well as the installation of insulation, are other effective retrofitting options.

- **Companies may reduce their air** - conditioning demands by increasing building envelope efficiency, using less power and being more effective simultaneously

- **Energy is a complex subject that affects every element of a structure** and poses a number of issues at the same time, such as energy prices, human comfort, and energy reliability. Facilities managers may have a major influence on energy efficiency of their systems integration by proactively monitoring equipment, efficiently employing control systems, and supporting programs to convert older buildings.

- **One of the known and most widely methods to save funds, reduce pollution, generate employment,** and lessen the rising energy demand is to use energy more effectively. When businesses invest in increasing their facilities' energy efficiency, they help to create a more sustainable future for people, organizations, and the ecosystem.

3.5 CONCLUSION

- **Building energy efficiency** has an important responsibility to contribute to energy security in growing economies, given the present rate of urbanization and the resulting growth in energy consumption. With the rising expense of new energy sources and the rising energy costs, authorities must shoulder the responsibility and cost of maintaining supply security with end-users by boosting efficiency **(Lemaire, 2008).**

- **New Avenues for energy savings have arisen** as a result of technological advancements in built environment and equipments. Moreover, many of these innovations have yet to be applied to African and other developing-country contexts, implying a significant savings possibility.

- **A Major obstacle is a lack of knowledge about building energy consumption** patterns and the alternatives and possibilities for energy reductions. Because of the expense of implementing energy reductions and the fear of change, there is likely to be any transition until a legal and regulatory system is established.

CHAPTER 4

4. GAINING INFLUENCE OF FACILITY MANAGEMENT

4.1 INTRODUCTION

Acceptance of the role of facilities management in business performance has gradually developed for profound change in the public sector and corporate world. The conception of Building Management has an indistinguishable connection with the idea of Facility Management. The planning of Facility Management starts along with the execution phase of the building. Based on the necessity for the building, the Facility Management scope can diverge in two main categories. These are:-

1. **Space and Infrastructure**

2. **People and Organization**

Facility Management regarding Space and Infrastructure deals with the hard services. These can be:-

- Space optimization and management

- Workplace management and optimization

- Technical management of building or property

- Management of energy

- Management of waste

- Outdoor and indoor cleaning

Facility Management regarding Space and Infrastructure deals with soft services. These can be:-

- Hygiene and Health

- Safety and Security

- Internal services

- Reception

- Meeting. etc.

- Internal logistics

- Mail service

- Transport service. etc.

4.2 ROLE OF FACILITY MANAGEMENT

- Architecture, Humanities, Technical Sciences, and Principles of business administration are all part of Facility Management according to International Facility Management Association.

- Large organizations are growingly accepting the relevance of Facilities Management (FM) in fulfilling organizational goals and objectives.

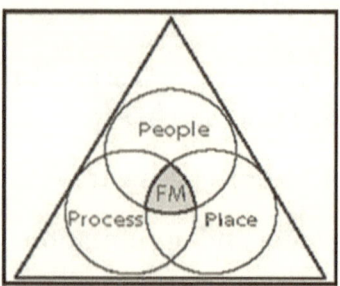

Figure 4.1   3p's and FM (Source: (Wahab & Kamaruzzaman, 2017))

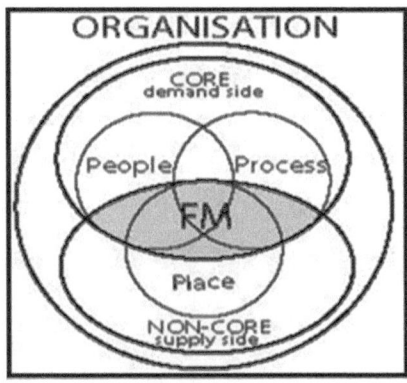

Figure 4.2   Demand - Supply and FM (source: (Wahab & Kamaruzzaman, 2017))

The above 2 figures depict the merger of people, process, and location in an organization that helps to advance the core and non-core business.

4.3   IMPORTANCE OF FACILITY MANAGEMENT

- **Facilities Management is a notion that is always evolving.** Facilities Management from the 1990's has emerged out of the integration of Building Maintenance Management with business aid services to become a elucidate zone in the management sector.

- **Computer-aided facility management** has provided effective information technology tools for mapping, evaluating, and managing facility management structures and processes since the 1990s.

- **One of the difficulties that Facility Managers** have is that they labor in continually converting circumstances. Non-core services such as payroll IT, which are traditionally not linked with this profession but are increasingly being addressed by FMs, are expected to grow in importance in the sector and its market.

- **The Modern concept of Facility Management is to ensure the building's long-term viability** by optimizing the layout and use of interior space, guaranteeing the functional and efficient operation of technological equipment, the quality of the internal environment, and other user requirements along with-it facility management also aim to create a high-quality interior environment while ensuring that the energy and resources need to run the building are used as efficiently as possible.

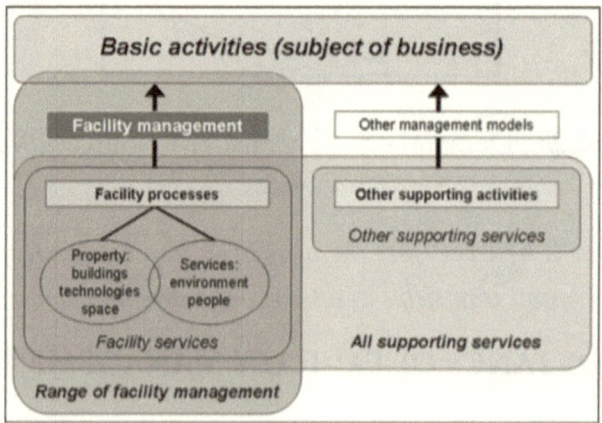

Figure 4.3 Facility Management structure and tasks and other assisting systems. (Source: (PAŠEK & SOJKOVÁ, 2018))

Facilities Management entails the following for the company:

- Establishing a facilities policy that reflects the company's values;

- Granting authority to the facilities management business unit to increase the quality of service;

- Constructing facilities to fulfill business needs objectives;

- Acknowledging the importance of facilities to the economy business.

4.4 SUSTAINABLE FACILITY MANAGEMENT

- **Society at large is putting growing pressure** on them to perform sustainably. With alarming legal urges and aims to combat global warming, FM is at the frontline of assembling national and international sustainability goals.

- **Sustainable Facilities Management has evolved** in tandem with the broader notion of sustainable development and a rising understanding of the magnitude of expected climate change. The facilities management profession has seized the objective for change and is trying to build practical sustainability goals within this quickly evolving field, which is both fortunate and appropriate.

- **As a result, the demand for sustainable facilities management**, as well as experienced facilities managers to carry out this duty, is increasing, as is the necessity to establish new ways of working to fulfill sustainability requirements. The current motivators are to address the obstacles of applying sustainable development excellence to facility management.

- **Facility Management influences on the natural environment** since it deals with the constructed environment and the processes that occur inside it. This point of interaction between the built and natural ecosystems is where sustainable facility management takes place.

The Buildings Ideal Performance depends mainly on:

- Physical Performance
- Functional Performance
- Financial Performance

*The term **"sustainable policy"** refers to a working document that has been authorized by an organization at the right level. It will provide direction and training on the best course of action from a variety of intertwined social, environmental, and economically viable practice options.*

Parts of the following procedures may be included in the implementation of a sustainability policy:

- Designing

- Selling

- Execution

- Target fixing

- Checking

- Surveying

- Assessing

The primary goal of a sustainability policy is to meet the assurance of an organization's stakeholders. For FM to accept innovation while offering a framework for commitment and advancement of sustainability, a comprehensive practice guide for implementing a sustainability policy would be critical. It is designed to assist FM practitioners in managing sustainability in the secondary processes that make up FM. Measure, monitor, declare and compete on defined Key Performance Indicators for long-term FM services management.

In FM, sustainability refers to a contribution to the long-term viability of a facility that is not owned by the FM provider but is managed and maintained by him. As a result, the notion of quantifying sustainability in FM emerges, along with a broad interface to current systems for facility sustainability evaluation.

At every stage of the building's life cycle, the Facility Management function must address the delicate interaction between constructed and natural surroundings. Sustainable Facility Management at every stage of the building's life plays a crucial part.

Inward Investment

- **The importance of Facilities Management in the economy is becoming more widely appreciated.** The establishment of the environment in which facilities management has arisen and is gaining momentum was influenced by key government policies in a market economy.

- **Some development organizations acknowledge the need for excellent facilities and property management for attracting inbound investment.** Inward investment is the infusion of funds into a region from outside sources to acquire capital goods for a corporation's branch to establish or expand its presence in the area.

- **Inward investment generates jobs and income in a region.** Facilities management is already regarded as an important factor in achieving economic success by many countries. Facilities management is viewed as a means to improve the efficacy of office workers as the reliance on workplace productivity grows.

- **Facilities help to attract inbound investment by providing the necessary infrastructure for the company.**

The Following are the Most Important facilities concerns for the future in all areas of the economy:

- Increasing the capacity to react to changing business requirements;

- Enabling creative individuals to operate in a healthy environment;

- Taking in the possibility of latest technologies;

- Maximizing the utilization of finite resources while reducing the negative environmental effect.

Facilities, like other corporate assets, are typically viewed as a capital investment that must be managed to increase and realize their worth. Organizations should do a basic assessment of how facilities are managed and the involvement they bring to the business to find possibilities and acknowledge their influence on the bottom line. Few people understand the importance of facilities as a **"factor of production,"** a means of establishing company identity, and a productive asset.

4.5   CONCLUSION

At every stage of the building's life cycle, the Facility Management function must address the delicate interaction between constructed and natural surroundings. Sustainable Facility Management at every stage of the building's life plays a crucial part.

It's both exciting and tough to identify the aspects that will have a long-term impact on the business in the dynamic and ever-changing world of facility management (FM), where the sector is still learning. Trends that are considered significant and game-changing today become a fad after a few months.

Facilities help to attract inbound investment by providing the necessary infrastructure for the company. Facilities, like other corporate assets, are typically viewed as a capital investment that must be managed to increase and realize their worth.

CHAPTER 5

5. OUTSOURCED SERVICES VS INHOUSE STAFF

5.1   INTRODUCTION

Facilities Management is all the work needed to be done to ensure smooth operation of a building or building complex. Facilities Management is important for well-being of the occupants of the building. It is a relatively new field in built environment. It is a unique discipline, and it informs us how a building is important for an organization's success in term of employees and customers satisfaction. The operation and management of facilities is a growing field which offers unique challenges to its workforce and in return, demands robust skills which need continually to be upgraded. As Facility Management is a relatively new field, people have arrived at their senior facility manager position through various ways and even accidentally.

Three General Categories of Work are:

1. **Building services:** technical, operational skills that keep building functioning.

2. **Space utilization**: layouts, fit-outs, relocations.

3. **Professional advisory:** translation, integration, alignment with business objectives.

These illustrate the scope and depth of knowledge needed to maintain and manage the built environment.

5.2 OVERVIEW

Facility management, like the word "sports," is a broad concept. Facility managers hold a title in the same way a sportsperson does, but their responsibilities and actions are as diverse as those of a sports icon. Anything from basketball and football to tennis and cricket can be found under the sports umbrella. The same can be said of various types of facilities managements.

There are several types of managed facilities, each with its own set of requirements and expectations.

Following are the nine core types of facilities managements:

1. Asset management and life cycle planning.

2. Emergency preparedness and continuity.

3. Employee satisfaction, health, and wellness.

4. Environmental stewardship and sustainability.

5. Interdepartmental communication.

6. Real estate and property management.

7. Space utilization and floor planning.

8. Technology and smart office planning.

9. Workplace leadership and strategy.

Facilities management can be done in two ways, by outsourcing facilities management and in-house facilities management.

The findings of some studies suggested that the goal of facilities management is to make the company's operations more effective. Facilities management concentrates on the capacity and efficiency of its working environment to support core operations, with the goal of achieving substantial value addition through successful planning and management. Most companies want to make the best value decision or get the best value for their money when it comes to their company or support services. "Both in house and outsource facilities management have unique abilities to contribute to the achievement of best value for money.

When an organization decides to outsource the services, they may have the opportunity to gain value for money and savings through lowering overhead costs (e.g., supervisions) and expenditure on other direct costs (e.g., plant and equipment)" (Myzatul Aishah Kamarazaly, 2007). This is due to the fact that an outsource business uses its own equipment and staff, and therefore runs the risk of inefficient equipment and resource utilization. Furthermore, by focusing on core operations, the company will be able to maintain its emphasis on its core strength and increase its competitive advantage (Singh, 2021).

5.3   OUTSOURCING DECISION CRITERIA

According to (Barker, 2013) when it comes to your employees' livelihoods, outsourcing services can be a delicate matter. It should always be approached with caution and carried out under the watchful eye of your entire department.

The decision to outsource a service or hire in-house workers should be based on strong reasoning and should consider the following factors (Barker, 2013).

- Does the service work; if it isn't broken, don't fix it!

- Does the service fit the requirements of the site?

- Is the service financially sound, or does it need a new financial model?

- Is there a sound reason for change?

Does the service work?

Do you welcome it when things change? One thing is certain: your employees will not. If you don't have a good, rational cause to mess with a system, leave it alone. A competent manager, on the other hand, is continually looking for ways to improve the service he or she delivers. You should evaluate your service on a regular basis to ensure that it continues to meet your operating needs.

- We already know how application of excellent customer service can modify operational requirements.

- Change for the sake of change is a poor approach to develop your team's working strategy, however attempting something new in short increments might be beneficial; if you don't test something, you'll never know if it works.

- Rather than approaching these tiny tweaks casually, you should build a strategy to deal with them.

- When it comes to how you should approach outsourcing vs. hiring in-house talent, the two are identical.

- You should not bring any service in-house without first doing some research to see what kind of service you'll get and whether it'll be better for your department and your client.

- If you start outsourcing your service, you may find that if it goes well, internal politics will make you want to outsource all of your operations. Change isn't always harmful, but it must be welcomed by your entire team from the beginning.

Does the Service Fit the Requirements of the Site?

- Your primary goal should always be to deliver the greatest service possible to the site. Only once you've gained a thorough understanding of your site can you decide whether the adjustments, you're considering are the greatest fit for it. The hope is that your company will continue to grow as a result of good, sound management techniques. All firms have a natural desire for this.

- Growth brings change, which is bound to have a number of consequences for your site and the services you provide. Waste and recycling, for example, become much larger concerns that need managerial and strategic decisions to deal with and stay within legal requirements. To ensure compliance, you may need to begin adding services that have never been required previously.

For Example, you may require a specific employee to handle waste or recycling. Alternatively, you may notice a synergy between roles, allowing you to combine roles to provide a more efficient service. Your site should take priority over your desire to build an empire. Any evaluation of a service must be based on facts and data rather than aspirations.

Is the Service Financially Sound?

- No Facilities Manager is fortunate enough to have an open cheque book for service supply. Your service offering must be based on sound financial judgments and forecasted outcomes. Although quality and service are crucial, they will not be successful if their application is not financially sound. However, there are occasions when services must be provided that are not financially sound.

- These are the services that help to improve an organization's image. These services, such as window cleaning, plant displays, and trash pick-up, must be clearly identified as areas that benefit an organisation. The image of an organisation, especially in educational institutions, should never be undervalued.

Is there a Sound Reason for Change?

• **Financial constraint, which is currently high on the list of every government-funded institution or group**, is one example of a problem that requires a change in how you do things. These boom-or-bust scenarios have occurred in the past and will most likely occur again in the future. An organization's response to these critical events can sometimes distinguish it from the other. Funding cuts might force change, which presents a problem for the Facilities Manager in terms of reducing services while maintaining compliance.

• **These judgments and decisions will be easier to make if a Facilities manager** thoroughly understands his or her organisation and the services supplied, and will, in the long run, result in a more robust organisation. The first reaction you are likely to have is indignation if you are asked to cut your budget and are expected to do so without compromising the services you provide.

• **The Assumption is that if you can lower your budget without sacrificing service,** you've been over-budgeting all along. The truth is that you should periodically re-evaluate your finances and services to ensure that you are not suffering from "service drift" (Barker, 2013).

5.4   ADVANTAGES

• **For a business, operational expenses are not the only thing to consider.** Other overhead costs, such as pensions, welfare benefits, extra office space, and other related expenses, could easily rise. It is best to restrict these expenses to the core staff of a business.

- **This can be done through outsourcing, as outsourcing allows a company** to benefit from economies of scale and cost structure, resulting in cost savings and a competitive advantage.

- **Since these are well-known organizations that perform these duties,** you are likely to come across specialists in these fields and activities.

- This way productivity of the company's team or the outsourced company is not affected by additional tasks or expenses.

- **The bulk of the work is passed on to experts as the small business's team focuses** on expanding its current scope.

- **Recruiting and recruiting highly qualified employees will necessitate the creation** of a human resources department, which a small business is unlikely to be able to do at this time.

- **Outsourcing such work allows you to narrow down your options to professionals** willing to work for the organisation at a lower cost than a typical employee in another department.

- **Outsourcing firms are specialists in their fields and have the expertise to meet your needs** in specific areas including customer service and marketing.

- **Companies may save the hassle of finding an expert by taking the help of an outsourcing** firm's geniuses to handle the rest.

- **The most significant advantage of outsourcing your critical business process is that employees** can concentrate on the core business process, spending its time doing what it is good at is more effective. However, there are many tasks that an organisation must complete for which it lacks skilled labour.

- **Perhaps a business is not very good at handling its finances, providing customer support,** or filling out all the necessary human resource paperwork. Any minute spent on tasks that are not part of a company's skill set is time wasted.

The core staff have more time to concentrate on Core Business Processes by outsourcing the day-to-day back-office activities. Anything beyond a company's core business operations is almost always more cost-effective to outsource. A company can save money, avoid tension, and focus all its resources on tasks for which they have skilled labor available (Singh, 2021).

5.5   DISADVANTAGES

- **Being unable to communicate with one another causes** company to function inefficiently as due to outsourcing the whole team is not working together in the same office and time zone, it's not easy to get changes in project done quickly because the majority of project communication takes place through written electronic means, such as email and not in person.

- **These forms of impersonal contact** do not have the same impact and may lead to misunderstandings or miscommunication.

- **When thinking of managing facility we should first understand** which method would be more suitable for particular facility, many people make decisions without proper understanding and analysis which might lead to bad decision.

- **The very first decision to make is to find out what will be more ideal** for specific facility in house facility management or outsourcing of facility management.

- **If we are intending to outsource facility then we should extensively explore** different facility management organizations and brief them about our requirements and consideration specials majors to be taken after that we should understand the offering and work pattern of different facility managers after considering major aspect and components, we should hire facility mangers who aligns with our requirements and will add value to facility.

- **Work pattern and cost of facility managements can differ according** to various markets for example places where outsourcing market is well developed and compatible with assets of various scale can create more awareness amongst people in regard to outsourcing which leads to more outsourcing of projects.

- **However, places where outsourcing market is less developed** seems to less known amongst people of subject of location in which most of them prefer to go for in house facility management because of cost saving but sometimes it can lead to miss management and work might not be on same level as the outsourcing partners as they hold expertise in facility management (Singh, 2021).

5.6 CONCLUSION

- **Outsourcing allows a company to take advantage of economies of scale** and a more cost-effective cost structure. Employees are able to focus on the core business process as a result of this. Outsourcing something other than core company processes is almost always more cost-effective.

- **A business can save money, reduce stress, and concentrate all of its energy on activities for which they have skilled labor available.** Although the small business's staff works on expanding its current scope, the majority of the work is passed on to experts.

- **The most important benefit of outsourcing your critical business process is that workers can focus on what they are good at,** which allows them to be more productive. By outsourcing day-to-day back-office tasks, the company can save time and money. It may also help to relieve stress and boost productivity.

- **The majority of project communication is done through written electronic means like email rather than in person.** These types of impersonal interaction do not have the same effect as personal contact and can lead to misunderstandings. After thoroughly studying research paper we have realized that Outsourcing is good in some cases and bad in some cases.

- **The Challenges of Outsourcing FM are ideal outsourcing partner,** suitability of outsourcing pertaining to various markets, quality of work, lack of control, language and cultural barrier (Singh, 2021).

6. FACILITY MANAGEMENT SOFTWARE

6.1 INTRODUCTION

- **The Facilities refers to the infrastructure including amenities at any property or built environment.** Thus, the management of facilities of any built environment is termed as Facility Management. All the infrastructures need manpower, material & other resources to maintain & operate it for the ease of users & in a cost-effective planning.

- **Facility Management acts as the function to achieve it.** Facility Management ensures right processes & practices, timely delivery, meeting compliances, right skill set & knowledge, to accomplish & deliver the assigned work. Thus, in turn it helps to minimize or eliminates the possibility of redo work, delayed responses or delayed completion of work, accidents, freedom from complaints, cost increase, decrease in operational life cycle of infrastructure & operational difficulties related to manpower.

- **The evolution of Facility Management Industry was considered during the early years 80's.** The Facility Management Industry started with concept of providing various services for a building or property. It started with outsourcing facility management services to external FM Company which included the technical & non-technical services or earlier called as hard & soft services.

- **This further groaned up with integration of more services & enabling technology for the services.** Later it evolved into integrated facility management, sustainable facility management & total facility management. Currently, it is also referred as Workplace Management.

6.2 FACILITY MANAGEMENT SOFTWARE

- **Facility management software is designed to simplify repair and maintenance programs by automating work orders,** facilitating preventive maintenance, and delivering a plethora of useful data about facility performance and spend. This sort of software is aimed to assist organizations save time and money by more efficiently and successfully managing their buildings, assets, and inhabitants.

- **Multi-site facility managers can perform a variety of functions related to ongoing maintenance and repair with a robust facilities management platform, including asset management,** commercial contractor sourcing and compliance, work order fulfilment, preventive maintenance scheduling, invoicing, and data analytics. FM teams can better track space usage, examine spending patterns over time, boost energy efficiency, and save expenses with the correct technologies, all while improving communication with service providers and internal stakeholders.

6.3 KEY BENEFITS OF FACILITIES MANAGEMENT SOFTWARE

A solid platform will help with a variety of jobs that are required to provide 24/7 brand support across all locations, as well as provide strategic insights into maintenance costs and resource allocation. Streamlined contractor invoicing and payment processing, enhanced insight into work order management, and increased access to facilities data are all key benefits of facilities management software:

a. **Repair & Maintenance Management:** Any FM team's major role is to keep assets in good operating order, which includes proactive scheduling of any essential repairs or maintenance (R&M). Work orders can be submitted on the move, their progress tracked, and their completion ensured with the correct software.

b. **Parts & Supply Management:** FM software makes it simple for firms to purchase approved sourced and contracted goods. Controlling these transactions allows companies to save money, verify quality, streamline ordering, and track warranties.

c. **Settlement/Payment Processing:** Contractor invoices can be submitted electronically, confirmed against negotiated rates and applicable sales taxes, tagged for G/L processing, and integrated with third-party accounting systems using facility management software.

d. **Asset Management:** FM software provides a single platform for storing a complete record of all equipment and locations, as well as all work history and maintenance information. This makes equipment warranties, mandatory inspections, and planned maintenance easier to tag, manage, and track.

e. **Proposal Management:** Most facilities management platforms include digital RFP management, which enables FMs to issue a Request for Proposal (RFP) to one or more vendors, track RFP status, and accept or sign contracts fast.

f. **Call Centre Access:** Call center access is common in facility management software, allowing location workers to submit work orders over the phone 24 hours a day, seven days a week. This enables official follow-up of time-sensitive service requests in order to assure timely contractor performance and, if necessary, reassignment.

g. **Contractor Sourcing and Management:** Through a single database, facility teams can find certified, verified, and insured contractors as well as all contractor data, such as W-9 forms and insurance information. This streamlines the contracting procedure while also ensuring higher-quality services at a reduced price.

h. **Preventive & Scheduled Maintenance:** The key to lowering R&M expenses is preventive maintenance. All preventative and scheduled facility maintenance events, including mandated inspections, can be scheduled, authorized not-to-exceed (NTE) price, and validated using FM software.

i. **Open and Scalable Architecture:** Facilities management software offered via the cloud or SaaS operates regardless of the underlying IT platform and is easily adaptable to company-wide system updates or modifications.

6.4 FACILITIES MANAGEMENT SOFTWARE FEATURES

a. **Simplified Work Order Management:** Work orders are subsequently routed to the relevant contractor at suitable, pre-approved prices, and location staff can enter facility maintenance service requests directly into the system.

b. **Staffing Support:** One-on-one assistance from Service Channel's experienced team for continuing solution updates and maintenance, contractor and site-specific location onboarding, and scalability as your company grows.

c. **Platform for Software as a Service (SaaS)** – Our cloud-based facilities management system eliminates costly software installs and upgrades, as well as the responsibility of managing additional hardware, lowering total cost of ownership considerably.

d. **Spend Analysis** — All spend data and analytics from facilities management are displayed in real time in easy-to-read dashboard graphics. Analyze historical data, spot trends and outliers, set targets and industry benchmarks, and anticipate future spending.

e. **Third-Party Integrations** — Service Channel's facility management software interfaces seamlessly to other business platforms including third-party accounting and payment systems, reducing data entry errors and streamlining payment and audit processes.

f. **Contractors can be easily found and vetted** — Maintain and update contractor contact and payment information, as well as track insurance and certifications, using simple, automated processes. Additionally, use our contractor directory to locate skilled service providers with the necessary capabilities for your project.

6.5 TYPES OF FACILITY MANAGEMENT SOFTWARE

Today's Market offers a variety of facilities management software options. **CAFM software (Computer-Aided Facility Management)** provides facilities managers with administrative functions such as tracking, management, planning, and reporting on physical spaces and company locations. **CAFM software** is typically used as a database for FM-related equipment, expenditures, and activities, and it frequently includes BIM or CAD capabilities.

Another type of facility management software is **CMMS (Computerized Maintenance Management Software)**, which has many of the same functions as **CAFM software** but gives a more in-depth look at a company's maintenance planning and execution. **CMMS software** may contain automated maintenance scheduling and tracking capabilities, and it is targeted toward preventive maintenance.

6.6   BUSINESSES CUT COSTS BY FM SOFTWARE

- **One of the quickest methods to cut facility management costs is to implement a software platform.** Simply switching from an error-prone, inefficient pen-and-paper system to a digitized, automated platform reduces the amount of time and resources allocated to work order administration, allowing teams to focus on proactive, preventive measures instead. Furthermore, having access to advanced analytics makes it simple to identify patterns of overspending and key areas for improvement, allowing them to be addressed and reversed swiftly.

- **Facility management software also connects with third-party financial systems**, allowing organizations to gain greater visibility into R&M spending while avoiding the time-consuming process of manual data entry. Businesses may get access to useful indicators like cost per square foot per year, cost per user, cost per workplace, cost per month, and a variety of additional statistics. This information aids facility managers in identifying areas for improvement and devising cost-cutting strategies.

- **Finally, the correct software makes implementing preventive maintenance programs much easier for enterprises.** Preventive maintenance saves money by lowering the number of failures and emergency repairs a company must deal with each year, as well as avoiding warranty lapses and unneeded equipment replacements. Assets will live longer with an automated preventive maintenance program in place, and overall maintenance costs will be significantly lowered.

6.7 ROI OF FACILITY MANAGEMENT SOFTWARE

- **Facility management software often provides a high return on investment, especially for multi-location organizations using pen-and-paper facilities programmers.** Often, the cost savings from converting to electronic payment processing (rather than manual invoicing) is sufficient to cover the cost of the program and then some.

- **Multiply your total yearly maintenance expense by the total annual savings percentage projected** as a result of the program implementation to get the possible ROI for facilities management software. This figure shows the total amount of money you'll save over the course of a year. To calculate the entire yearly ROI savings, subtract the cost of the FM software from the total annual efficiency savings.

6.8   CONCLUSION

The issue over the use of facility management software has already been settled, with the recognition that it is more accurate and has superior record-keeping capabilities than a paper-based system. There are numerous articles and blog posts on the internet that describe the main elements of facility management software (FMS) that assist an organisation in working successfully, efficiently, and effectively.

Office space planning, control, and monitoring have become a critical aspect of good business administration as individuals all around the world attempt to react to the uncertainties of COVID-19. Many firms were forced to transition to remote work options because of the pandemic, which has since become a mainstay of modern workplace culture. Prior to the epidemic, working from home was frequently promoted as a benefit to attract and retain top talent. However, with more than two-thirds of organizations expecting to reopen offices this summer, hybrid onsite and remote work may become the norm, necessitating a rethinking of your current space management techniques.

7. FACILITIES MANAGEMENT IN INDIA

7.1 INTRODUCTION

- **The Indian Facilities Management (FM)** sector is undergoing fast changes in end-user industries, which has resulted in a significant increase in commercial activity in major cities such as Delhi/NCR, Mumbai, Hyderabad, Pune, Chennai, and Bengaluru. According to a Technavio report, the FM Industry's predicted **CAGR for the next three years is 17.19 percent.**

- **The unorganized sector still makes up the bulk of the Indian market; however,** due to the rising effect of urban growth, post-modernization, and the RERA act, the industry is currently moving toward a more organized approach. FM services are, in effect, gradually increasing appeal among both commercial and residential consumers.

- **The government's newly stated intention to build 100 smart cities is a strong sign of the country's development prospects in the FM arena,** as it now extends beyond Tier I cities. This strategy is projected to result in a spike in infrastructure investments (almost $200 billion), necessitating the need for professional FM services.

- **The majority of the newly created industry is planned to be built around the concept of smart cities.** With people's tastes increasingly moving towards a safer, cleaner, and more secure environment, the country's real estate boom is projected to accelerate. With the country's IT boom and E-commerce investments from businesses like Amazon and Alibaba, the general requirement for infrastructure and well-organized places is only going to grow, which bodes well for FM's future. (silagroup.co.in)

7.2 MARKET OVERVIEW AND INSIGHTS OF FM INDUSTRY IN INDIA

Over the projected timeframe, the Indian Facilities Management Market is expected to grow at a CAGR of 24%. (2021 - 2026). The Indian market for facility management services is projected to be driven by a rising focus on outsourcing non-core functions and expansion in the real estate industry. **Along with this, the market is likely to be driven by government regulations on safety measures and environmental concerns to adopt green practices** (*www. mordorintelligence.com*).

- **The facilities management industry in the** nation is fragmented since most sites in the country operate on in-house administration and building management systems.

- **India has a flourishing service industry that absorbs a large amount of international capital.** According to IBEF, the country's IT companies made the most money in fiscal 2018, bringing in USD 167 billion. The country's organised industries are projected to develop as a result of government measures. The economy is likely to play a key role in channelling foreign investment and influencing the market throughout the projection period.

- **The upsurge in the country of outsourcing non-core functions is projected to boost demand for Facilities Management.** The Somnath Temple in Gujarat was recently named the cleanest temple in India as part of the Swachh Bharat Mission, and BVG India Ltd is responsible for its upkeep.

- **The market is being driven by government safety requirements and a focus on green practices** over environmental issues across the country. The Ministry of Labor and Employment's Occupational Safety, Health, and Working Conditions Code, 2019, is anticipated to encourage businesses to use facility management services so they may focus on their main activities.

The COVID-19 pandemic is still transforming the growth of numerous industries; nevertheless, the outbreak's immediate impact varies. COVID-19 will have a negligible impact on India's facilities management services sector. According to Technavio's pandemic industry analysis, market growth would likely increase in 2021 over 2020. According to new research from Technavio, the facility management services market size in India in the environmental & facilities services industry is predicted to expand by USD 13.43 billion between 2021 and 2025, at a CAGR of about 14%.

India's Market for Facility Management Services Key Highlights for the Environmental and Facilities Services Industry in 2021-2025:

- During the projected period 2021-2025, the market is expected to grow at a compound annual growth rate of 5%.

- Future trends and shifts in consumer behaviours are forecasted.

- In India, the market for facility management services is growing at a rapid pace.

7.3 KEY MARKET TRENDS AND MAJOR PLAYERS

- **The Market is expected to be driven by steady growth in the real estate sector**. The real estate industry is being driven by rising earnings and urbanization because of the country's economic progress. According to IBEF, the country's real estate sector attracted USD 30 billion in institutional investments between 2009 and 2018. In addition, the government enables 100 percent foreign direct investment in township and settlement development projects, which is projected to boost the market.

- **One of the Factors propelling the market is the rising demand for office space in the country;** according to Money control, office leasing surpassed 30 million sq ft in the first half of 2019. The demand for facility management is likely to rise as the number of offices grows.

- **The Number of flexible workspaces in the country is increasing, and the convenience and cost-effectiveness of co-working spaces are luring small and medium-sized businesses in**. According to NAREDCO, the co-working category has taken up 6.9 million square feet from fiscal 2017 to the first quarter of 2019.

- **Facility management services are also becoming increasingly popular in the residential real estate market**. The market is driven by the country's expanding number of residential buildings. ('india-facility-management-market @ www.mordorintelligence. com')

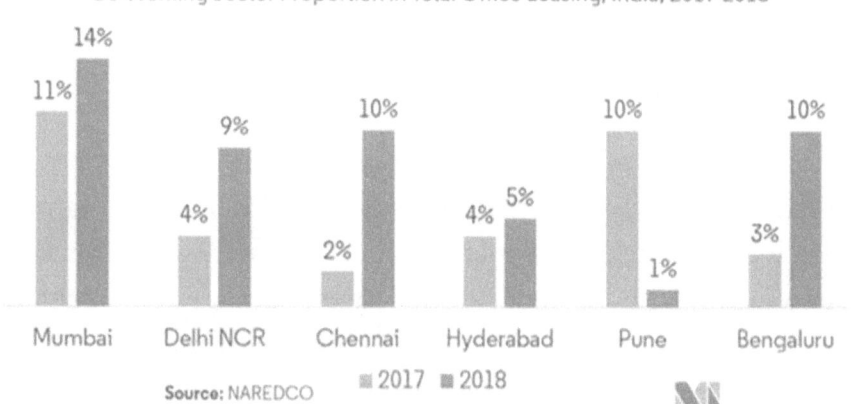

Figure 7.1 Co-Working Sector Proportion

Image Source: www.mordorintelligence.com

7.4 MARKET SNAPSHOT AND KEY MARKET PLAYERS

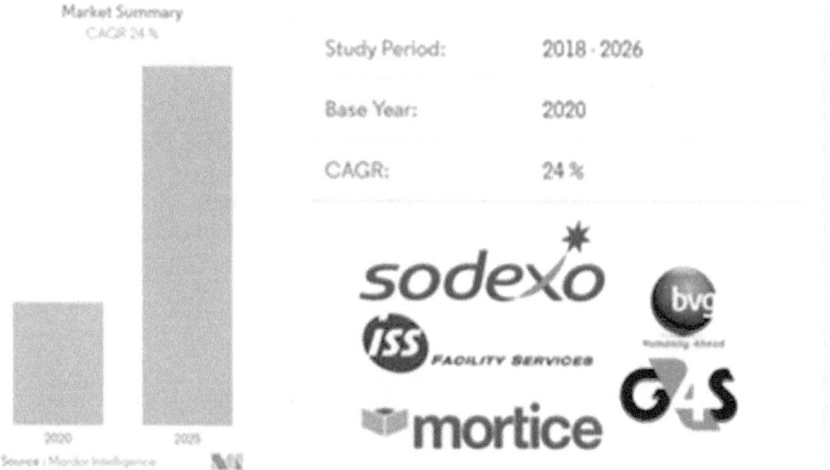

Figure 7.2 Market trend

Image Source: www.mordorintelligence.com

7.5 FM SERVICES IN INDIA/ INNOVATIVE MODULES

Growing Demand

In India, the in-house segment dominates this market however, these services are rapidly being outsourced. The industry's growth is also being fueled by the increased demand for integrated facility management. With the industry rapidly migrating to the organized sector, the integrated sector is likely to grow even more. While the market is currently highly fragmented and dominated by unorganized small operators, it is likely to grow more organized in the future years as larger players acquire smaller players. In India, the commercial sector is the most popular industry, followed by the industrial and other sectors. (*Www.Mordorintelligence.Com.*) Corporate offices, such as those in the IT, BPO, and BFSI sectors, are increasingly migrating their services to outsourcing, resulting in industry growth in India. Tier 1 and metro cities are the most densely populated areas in the sector. Within the industry, Pune and Mumbai are projected to see significant expansion.

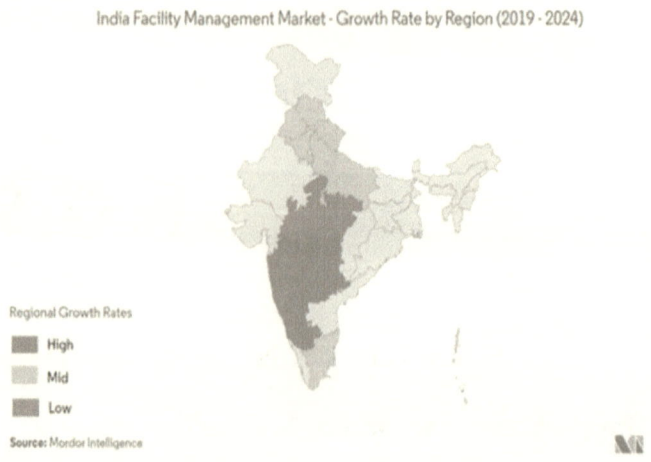

Figure 7.3 India Facility Management Market-Growth Rate by Region (2019-2024)

7.6 EXAMPLES OF SOME INNOVATIVE MODULES BY A FM COMPANY

BIM for FM:

- (facilityexecutive.com') Contractors and Architects utilize Building Information Modelling (BIM) to create and scale virtual models of construction projects. Prior to construction, BIM provides building owners and operators with a complete visual representation of their facilities. While BIM is not a new technology, it is only now beginning to gain traction in the field of facility management.

- The Value of these solutions for project delivery and data accessibility is being recognized by facility operators. When O&M manuals, floor plans, and asset information relate to existing work order programs or facility maintenance software, facility teams benefit from increased access to O&M manuals, floor plans, and asset information. While still in its infancy, firms are seeing the potential for visual modelling to increase collaboration and communication among construction teams.

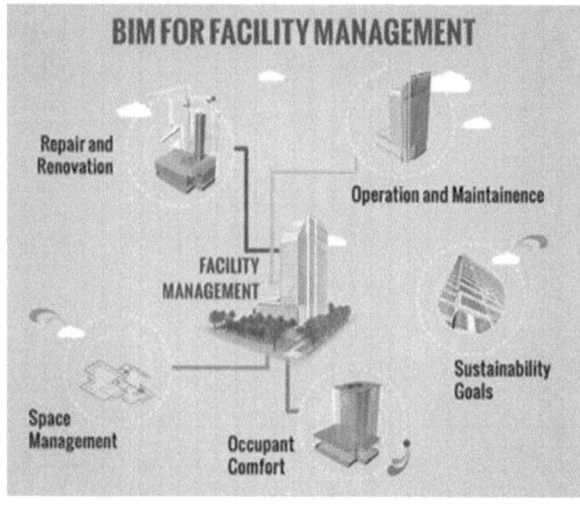

Figure 7.4   BIM and FM

1. **The Internet of things (IOT) in FM:**

   - **The Internet of Things (IoT) refers to your facility's network of internet-connected gadgets.**

   - **Sensors, thermostats, and actuators** are utilized on the Internet of Things to evaluate data and reduce the amount of energy used for tasks.

   - **Each Sensor or gadget collects data** about a building to better tell a facilities staff about current temperature, light, vibration, and even sound levels in certain regions.

Figure 7.5   IoT in FM

2. **HVAC**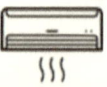

   - **The HVAC System** is particularly expensive technology to use and maintain in large establishments. Technology and the use of "Green" ideas have aided in the improvement of HVAC systems.

- **Being Able to lower your facility's heating and cooling costs** while also lowering your carbon impact is a win-win situation for everyone.

- **Building Automation systems (BAS) and HVAC facility management** technologies have come a long way in lowering facility management expenses.

- **These Programs save money** for facility managers by alerting maintenance crews when systems aren't working properly.

  This allows building managers to prevent costly equipment failure by resolving issues before they arise

Figure 7.6   HVAC Control

3. **Automated Facility Management Software**

- Without facility maintenance software, facility managers are forced to rely on spreadsheets, paper designs, or their own expertise, wisdom, and memory to keep their facilities running.

- Undocumented information will cause problems, especially if one facility manager leaves and is replaced.

- This lack of facility management technologies might have a negative influence on the structure and result in more costly repairs. Existing paper-based work orders may result in data entry duplication.

4. **Drones in FM**

- Drones offer amazing prospects for facilities management efficiency.

- The most promising applications for these unmanned aerial vehicles (UAVs) are in the areas of safety and automation.

- Roof inspections after a hailstorm, for example, will be coordinated by groups of drones following pre-programmed GPS routes. Having team members climb on facility roofs with a clipboard and camera to document damage is no longer necessary. (facilityexecutive.com')

Figure 7.7   Perfect tool for Facility inspection

7.7   INDUSTRY CHALLENGES

(Santhosh Upadhay) One of the main issues the sector is now facing is a lack of technical and non-technical manpower. Due to a shortage

of skilled personnel, mobilizing resources/staff once a project has been successfully contracted has taken longer.

- **Many clients have been pushed to replace long-term contracts** with medium-term contracts due to rising inflation and labor costs.

- **Many clients prefer to keep medium- and short-term contracts** rather than long-term contracts because the latter will result in a price increase.

- **Competition is the next major issue that acts as a barrier.** Because the market is flooded with low-cost unorganized service providers, pricing and margins are squeezed as these unorganized firms offer services at low prices, thus suffocating large, organized players.

- **Many multinational property management organizations,** on the other hand, have entered this sector and have seen tremendous growth over the previous five years. Because the construction industry is seeing an increase in expenditures across vertical sectors, new entrants, primarily from the United States and the United Kingdom, are projected to boost competitiveness in the future.

- **Due to high entry hurdles, joint ventures (JV) are seen as a deterrent factor.** JVs would make it easier for market participants to provide easy access to their client networks, enhance personnel strength, broaden their service portfolio, and expand their regional footprints to raise brand awareness.

- **Few New or Established FM firms are considering collaborating** with or acquiring a local firm to join or develop into this sector.

7.8 GROWTH OPPORTUNITIES

(Santhosh Upadhay) Because of the increased maturity of end users and the demand for improved safety, comfort, and expert asset care, the outlook for FM services in India is looking bright. The presence of global and Indian MNCs in various end-user sectors is primarily driving the FM services market in India, as they are potential clients due to their improved awareness levels, desire to invest and exposure to facilities.

- **Due to the current expansion and increase in investments in the Indian IT/Its/BPO and finance/banking sectors,** the IT sectors are more worried about individualized and specialized services utilizing both hard and soft services. Increased investment from developing sectors like as health care, retail, and infrastructure are predicted to propel this market to a higher growth curve later in its life cycle.

- **Because the market is still in its early stages of development, with little penetration of the outsourcing idea, the public sector, notably government offices, industrial, and educational segments, offer extremely limited possibility.** Only the soft services are primarily outsourced to local FM firms. The end-user sectors' expansion of business activities in tier 2 and tier 3 cities is seen as a rising regional growth trend for the FM services market in India. FMCG companies should be able to overcome competition and take use of the numerous chances available in stores. Simultaneously, India's FM market is adopting a more structured strategy in order to attain more market penetration and maturity.

- **Many organizations have used inorganic growth techniques to enter the market by acquiring well-established firms in order to gain a significant part of the industry.** Companies are always looking for new ways to expand and adapting their company models to meet consumer demands. A2Z Group, based in India, bought IPMSL and CNCS Facility Solutions, among other recent / large acquisitions.

- **Second, the Compass Group of the United Kingdom purchased India's Vipul Facilities Management** and Ultimate Hospitality Services, while Tenon Property Services enlarged its portfolio as Peregrine Guardine, Roto Power, and Mortice Group were all acquired.

7.9   CONCLUSION

(Santhosh Upadhay)The IT/ITeS sector was the first to outsource these services. As a result, a greater emphasis on commercial areas such as IT/I TeS/BPOs/Finance/Banking is advocated, as these will drive future demand for outsourced services. It's also a good idea to target businesses like **oil and gas, power, petroleum, steel, cement, pulp and paper, pharmaceuticals, and automobiles because they're already aware of the notion and are aware of the advantages of outsourcing.**

- **The Two Most Essential primary success criteria for an FM service provider in determining the company's success rate are brand visibility and competitive pricing;** vital industry relationships can also be utilized by participating in/ organizing major events and conferences. The influence of the real estate developer on the FM service provider is significant.

- **To implement an FM project, it is therefore recommended to have a regular relationship or to establish a tie-up with a civil contractor / real estate developer.** This will add value by making marketing easier and ensuring a higher selling price for the home. Due to the high entry barriers and fragmented nature of the industry, joint ventures with a local FM firm are encouraged in order to understand the local rules and variations in client preferences, as well as to sustain local competition because local companies are given significant preference.

- **The FM industry is about to move into the development stage of the market life cycle.** Participants in the industry are seeking for new ways to increase their business. The market is expected to grow at a phenomenal rate, providing FM enterprises with a significant growth opportunity. End users like the experience and these suppliers can provide a competent service, therefore demand for both hard and single services is projected to stay robust.

8. GLOBAL PRESENCE

8.1 INTRODUCTION

(www.highspeedtraining.co.uk') While the nature of the job varies by industry, facilities management is always necessary. Facilities management, according to the British Standards Institution, is "the integration of procedures inside an organisation to maintain and develop agreed-upon services that support and improve the effectiveness of its principal activities."

A facilities manager, to put it another way, oversees the day-to-day organisation and delivery of services on behalf of your company. The position's goal is to lower your company's outgoing costs while still guaranteeing that it accomplishes all its goals.

8.2 IMPORTANCE OF FACILITIES MANAGEMENT WORLDWIDE

Facilities management is an essential component of running a successful company.

As a result, incorporating a facilities manager into your business's day-to-day operations will be critical to:

Strategic Planning:

Strategic planning gives your company a clear direction and allows you to track success over time. From where you are now to where you want to be, strategic planning will help you get there.

As a result, strategic planning is critical to your company's continued success and manageability.

1. **Managing daily operations:**

   - Ordering stock could be one of the responsibilities.

   - Assuring that all facilities follow the rules and regulations.

   - Central services such as reception, mail, cleaning, waste disposal, and recycling are planned, directed, and coordinated.

   - Keeping employees safe

2. **Implementing health and safety procedures:**

   Procedures must be in place to ensure that all employees, visitors, and members of the public are safe. This is usually handled by the facilities manager. To limit the dangers of workplace hazards, they will conduct risk assessments and create and enforce health and safety procedures.

3. **Organizing maintenance, repairs and security of the building and premises:**

   Facilities managers are typically in charge of your building's security, maintenance, and repairs. This safeguards employees and their belongings, prevents unauthorized entry, and guarantees that your building complies with all legal standards. Facilities managers are responsible for overseeing the entire site, or a specific section of it, assessing its state, determining whether repairs are required, and ensuring that these repairs are completed.

8.3 VARIOUS ACCREDITATIONS

1. **Facility Management Professional Certification:**

   The Facility Management Professional® (FMP) certification is offered by the International Facility Management Association (IFMA) and is designed for entry-level and transitioning facilities professionals who want to improve their maintenance skillset and gain immediate credibility with employers, clients, and peers.

2. **Certified Facility Manager Credential:**

   The CFM certificate, which is also given by the International Facility Management Association, is one of the most well-respected qualifications in the facility management sector. This certification is indicated for experienced facility managers with at least 5 years of field experience. It is designed to measure professionals' expertise in the area through both work experience and study.

3. **Sustainability Facility Professional Certification:**

   The Sustainability Facility Professional (SFP), which is also offered by the International Facility Management Association as an assessment-based program that helps professionals understand how sustainable maintenance can positively impact an organization's triple bottom line – profit, people, and the environment.

4. **LEED Certification:**

   The Leadership in Energy and Environmental Design (LEED) certification program is a globally recognized green building certification program. LEED is a framework developed by the

United States Green Building Council (USGBC) to help building owners and operators recognize and implement sustainable maintenance, energy management, construction, and operations.

5. **Facilities Management Certificate by BOMI International:**

   This Facilities Management Certificate (FMC) is offered by BOMI International, a company that offers a variety of courses and programs for people who work in property management or facility management and want to further their education.

   The FM certificate program includes all of the important topics in the field of facility maintenance. You must complete three courses to get the FM certification: Fundamentals of Facilities Management; Design, Operation, and Maintenance of Building Systems (parts I and II). (limblecmms.com)

8.4   USE OF INTEGRATED FM GLOBALLY

- **(www.prnewswire.com) From USD84.65 billion in 2020 to USD114.86 billion in 2026,** the global integrated facility management market is expected to increase. Due to the requirement for a decent working environment and lower energy output costs, the need for standardization and simplification of facilities in businesses and residential buildings is predicted to increase in the future years, positively influencing the Global Integrated Facility Management Market.

- **Type, Services, IT (Information Technology)** support, solution, end-user, and region are all segments of the global integrated facility management market. The market may be divided into two types: hard service and soft service, with the hard service segment accounting for roughly 55 percent of the market in 2020 due to increased investments in energy and project management to achieve long-term efficiency. Furthermore, the market is expected to be driven by new office buildings in emerging economies during the forecast period.

- **North America,** with a value share of roughly 44 percent in 2020, was the greatest contributor to the Global Integrated Facility Management Market. In 2020, the United States was the region's greatest contributor, accounting for roughly 83 percent of total contributions, followed by Canada and Mexico. Furthermore, as a result of increased awareness and better economies, the need for outsourced facility management services is growing in developing countries.

- **JLL Inc (Jones Lang LaSalle IP, Inc),** ISS A/S (International Service System), CBRE Group Inc, Cushman & Wakefield plc, Sodexo Inc., Compass Inc., Aramark Corporation, Coor Service Management Holding AB, Mitie Group PLC, MacLellan Integrated Services, Inc. are the leading players in the Global Integrated Facility Management Market. To grow a customer base, market participants are always delivering services with real-time response, connectivity, and availability 24 hours a day, seven days a week.

8.5 DIFFERENT CHALLENGES FACED

1. **Improving Space Utilization:**

   Poor space usage can cost a large company hundreds of thousands of dollars per year. Many facility managers and corporate real estate executives, on the other hand, have no notion how much space is being squandered across their portfolio. One major cause is the lack of uniform space categorization in different locales. Another issue is a lack of visibility caused by a lack of or heterogeneous space management software system (www.iofficecorp.com).

2. Managing Workplace Technology:

As a company grows, so does its technological infrastructure. Facilities management leaders at each location or region will most likely choose technology based on personal preference or recommendations from others if no standards have been set. And before you know it, you've got three distinct space management software systems, seven different service request systems, and dozens of additional disparate solutions. Terms, capabilities, user interfaces, logins, and monthly invoices are all different. This is not only a stressful experience for company facilities managers, but it can also lead to a lot of waste and duplication. Only by conducting an enterprise-wide inventory and appointing one person (or, more likely, a committee) to assess them all can these lost technology costs be avoided.

3. Managing Meeting Rooms:

The larger your company, the more meetings you'll have at any given time—and the more meeting rooms you'll need to coordinate. But just because your firm is expanding doesn't mean you should be searching for a room or holding conference calls in closets.

4. Managing Facility Maintenance:

It's difficult enough to manage facility maintenance for several buildings. It's considerably more difficult if you have multiple ticketing systems for various types of service requests and facilities. Fortunately, this is simple with the appropriate facility management software. All service requests can be viewed by enterprise facilities managers on a single, mobile-friendly portal. They can also delegate tasks to their staff, monitor progress, and receive automatic warnings when preventative maintenance is due.

5. **Planning moves and expansion:**

When your company is rapidly expanding, you must be able to plan for long-term expansion while also making swift office relocation. Many businesses struggle with this because they are too big to respond quickly.

6. **Helping Employees Navigate the Workplace:**

Employees must be able to navigate a large corporate campus swiftly and easily in addition to having the relevant information at the right time. This is a big challenge for enterprise firms.

Employees can identify people and get turn-by-turn directions to their next meeting using wayfinding software, digital signs, and workplace apps. This reduces friction and stress throughout their day, allowing them to concentrate on the task at hand. (@ www. iofficecorp.com)

8.6 CONCLUSION

Geographically, the Facility Management Market is divided into **North America, South America, Europe, Asia Pacific, and the Middle East and Africa.** The North American region, which includes the **United States, Canada, Mexico, and Costa Rica,** is studied because it is usually the market's hotspot. The continent of South America is further divided into **Brazil, Argentina, Chile, Columbia, and a few more** developing countries are among them.

The market in Europe is thoroughly investigated, with the **United Kingdom, Germany, France, Italy, Spain, the Netherlands, Poland, Switzerland**, and a few more promising economies included.

CHAPTER 9

9. ARTIFICIAL INTELLIGENCE (AI)

9.1   INTRODUCTION

In the current world, the **Focus of FM** is on modifying corporate strategy and atmosphere developments, with a strong focus on the framework for developing and implementing business and assist models that are aligned with current market trends in *Corporate Real Estate, Facility Management, Workplace Solutions, Connectivity, Ecological, Sustainable, Health, Safety, Innovation, Global Trends, and Industry Benchmarking Practices.* Facility management is regarded as a business facilitator, with the goal to provide value, introduce innovation, supporting fundamental business objectives, and maximizing practical use of the physical environment. The introduction of novel digital technology and solutions is helping to improve the facility's strategic plan and activities substantially.

9.2   IMPORTANCE OF TECHNOLOGY

The internet of things (IoT), robotic process automation (RPA), artificial intelligence (AI), smart building/smart workplace detectors and surveillance, and digitalization are all transforming employment. The Internet of Things (IoT) involves the collection and use of data created by implanting sensors, and other physical items over a shared network. With the aid of technology, the usage of IoT devices and sensors is quickly expanding. The way we design, plan, and operate facilities is also evolving as a result of technological advancements. System reactions and repairs may be flagged and prioritized using cloud-based managing systems that collect data from different equipment and facilities. IoT is opening up a slew of new possibilities for innovative applications that may both make our lives better and boost business efficiency. **Finally, these new technologies can help enterprises focus on strategic roles rather than tedious activities.**

9.3   USE OF SENSORS

The Internet of Things (IoT) is a concept that brings technology into human daily life. The notion of safety and privacy has become one of the key categories in which technology benefits us. A smart home is made up of computers, smartphones, and other smart sensors or actuators via an IoT interface.

IoT is a network of interconnected smart devices that transfers data without needing engagement between both the user and the computer. This offers a platform for a surveillance system by allowing the user to experience comfort at home and leave the house ensuring that they'll be notified if somebody approaches the house. The notion of safety and security is one area where the technology may help us.

The fact that the vast majority of our population now carries technology on their person, as opposed to prior years of smartphones, makes the idea of cellphones acting as a security warning system more enticing. Individuals may now check house/office/store security situations on constantly because of the recent growth in accessibility and use of sensible IoT systems and the accessibility of mobiles. By using the IoT alert system to take photos depending on movements, it will grasp to distinguish between someone who is permitted to enter the smart home and someone who is not.

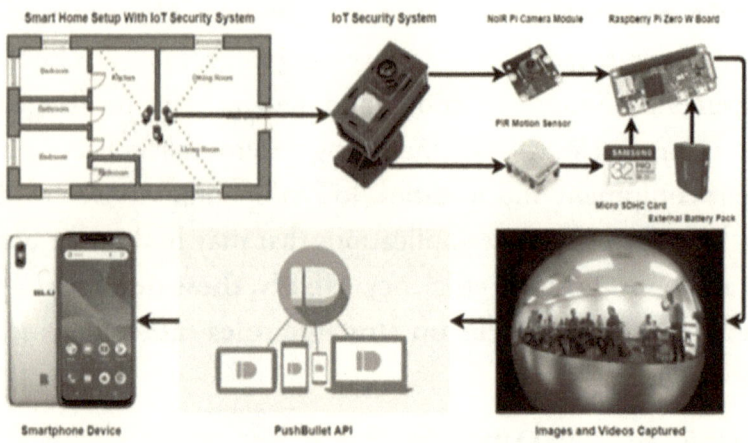

Figure 9.1 An effective security system ((Majumder & Izaguirre, 2020)

9.4 AI FOR CONSTRUCTION

Artificial intelligence is projected to boost productivity across the whole value chain, from building materials manufacturing to drafting, designing, and execution, as well as facility management.

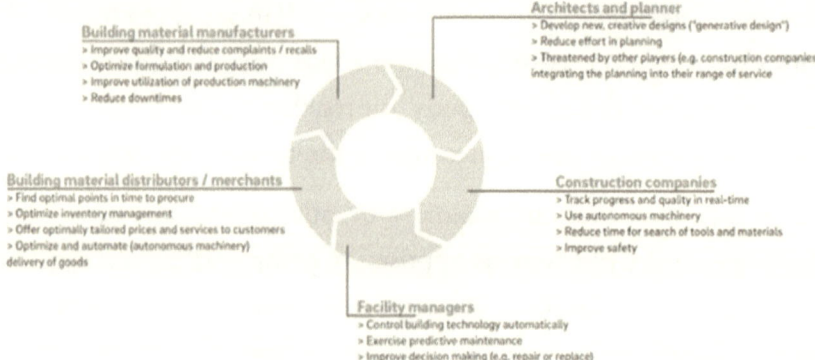

Figure 9.2 How AI can help different stake holders (Source: (Schober, 2020))

9.5   AI FOR DECISION MAKING

- **For a long time, the construction sector** has been cautious to adopt new technology. Individuals in the real estate development sector rely significantly on transferring skills from one operation to the next. This personnel learns how to handle hazards associated with property acquisition, but after they retire, this expertise is lost.

- **When it comes to land acquisition,** an AI-based decision-support system that considers the risks and the market may learn from each project and apply what it has learned to future initiatives. Artificial intelligence in facility management might enhance the accuracy of personnel distribution in current operations.

- **Employees in facility management might benefit** from an AI-based assist system that shows them where building help from workers is required. This sort of technology might aid workers in saving time and increasing efficiency.

- **Artificial Intelligence (AI) could be the alternative** in that it could enhance industrial operational planning by constantly detecting variations, keep all project participants aware of potential changes, and improve productivity.

- **BIM (Building Information Model)** is the most common use of AI in construction today. As there is less ambiguity, using support while making judgments can assist managers in making more conscious choices. The decision-making system accumulates essential facts and serves as a foundation for the choice.

- **The organization or an individual making a specific choice** might utilize this decision foundation. Because of the quantity of knowledge evaluated, the system may provide a more holistic perspective by analyzing a large amount of data.

- **This method can provide information to the decision-maker** about the dangers that their decisions may entail. When a firm in the construction sector buys property to develop on, there are several risks to consider. These dangers might be market-related, technological, or legal in nature.

- **A shift in demand and popularity, for example,** might constitute a market-related risk. The technical risk might be related to the project's complexity, while the legal risk could be related to unexpected twists.

9.6 SCOPE AND FUTURE OF AI

Although a slow initial acceptance rate, building executives are becoming more interested in AI technology's revolutionary potential. AI can also help operators of heavy and mobile gear on construction sites. AI has the potential to change the lives of millions of people if we are patient enough to fine-tune the user experience and achieve product-market fit. Technology has been progressively employed in a variety of ways to make building more efficient and inventive in recent years. Flying a drone over a building site, optimizing shift patterns to increase safety regulations, or selecting the optimum setting based on forecasts are no longer unusual. All of this is feasible because of AI. Expect a faster rate of tech adoption in the future years as more applications and solutions aimed at the construction industry become available.

Cost Savings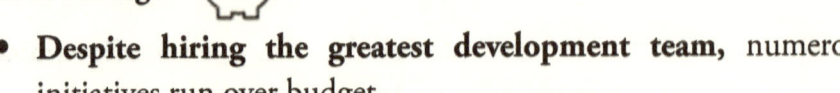

- **Despite hiring the greatest development team,** numerous initiatives run over budget.

- **Artificial Neural Networks (ANNs)** are employed on projects to predict budget overruns depending on criteria such as the size of the project, type of contract, and project management skill.

- **AI has been shown to aid effectively manage** schedules for future work by using predictive modeling and previous data, as well as links to scheduling systems and other related information.

- **Planned analytics can prevent you from getting expensive** disruptions and interruptions. As a consequence, project completion is accelerated.

Safety Audits Can Be Automated

- **Construction is fraught with dangers.** At the site, there are several possible risks, ranging from hazardous buildings to working machinery that poses a threat to people.

- **AI is already assisting in the improvement** of the whole job site safety.

- Construction sites are increasingly being outfitted with cameras, IoT devices, and sensors that successfully manage elements of construction activities and alert personnel when prospective safety concerns are detected.

- **This automatic function may be run every minute** and will log any potentially dangerous occurrences. It may also be used to train a picture prediction model to identify the sort of activity being carried out, such as bar bending, concreting, and so on.

- **This also lowers risk,** but it also has the potential to help and improve capability.

Routine Tasks Execution

- **At construction Sites, AI can also help operators of huge and movable equipments.** When working with a machine, operators frequently do many activities at once. As a result, there is a high rate of mistakes and inefficiency.

- **By Aiding the machine operator in performing regular activities,** AI has the prospective to greatly improve the utilization of heavy machinery.

- **Because AI-based technologies can quickly learn and adapt to these repetitious activities**, they are well-suited to be replaced by them. The operator can then focus on more difficult activities.

Resource retrenchment

- **AI additionally aids in the further optimization** of logistics based on the itineraries.

- **Based on data on times and dates, traffic, addresses, revenue, speed, and other factors, artificial intelligence** calculates the optimal mode of transportation as well as the best routes.

- **Furthermore, with each delivery completed, it enhances its suggestions.** These routes will be utilized by autonomous transportation modes such as trucks, vehicles, aircraft, and ships in the future.

Post-Construction

- **Long after the work is finished,** building managers can employ AI.

- **Advanced analytics and AI-powered algorithms** provide important insights into the operation and performance of a building, bridge, roads, and practically anything in the built environment by gathering information about a structure using sensors, drones, and other wireless technologies.

- **This implies AI may be used to track the progression of issues,** decide when a constructive repair is required, and even manage individual interactions for maximum safety and security.

9.7 CONCLUSION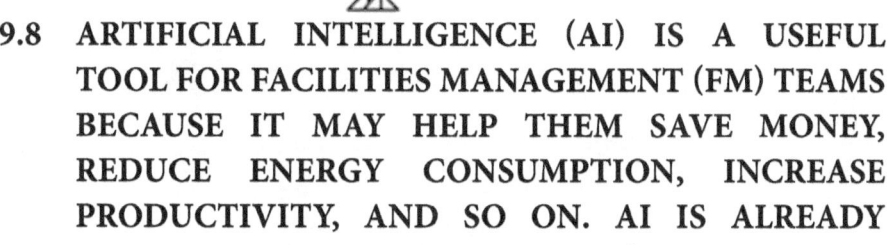

9.8 ARTIFICIAL INTELLIGENCE (AI) IS A USEFUL TOOL FOR FACILITIES MANAGEMENT (FM) TEAMS BECAUSE IT MAY HELP THEM SAVE MONEY, REDUCE ENERGY CONSUMPTION, INCREASE PRODUCTIVITY, AND SO ON. AI IS ALREADY HAVING A POSITIVE IMPACT ON FM TEAMS AND COMPANIES AS A WHOLE BY:

1. Increase cost savings and decrease energy usage.

2. Focus on predictive maintenance.

3. Reduce the potential for human error.

4. Streamline the integration of the IT, FM, and HR departments.

5. Improve building security and protocol.

The Possibilities for facilities management with AI technology are expanding at a rapid pace. The possibilities with AI are infinite, from enhancing productivity and efficiency to executing jobs like virtual office tours. However, all of this new technology might be intimidating.

AI may be integrated into your company in whatever capacity you choose and taken from there. If you're interested in learning more about AI but aren't sure where to begin, start small. Perhaps starting with an integrated workplace management system that streamlines office processes and working your way up from there.

CHAPTER 10

10. CASE STUDY-SUCCESS

An Integrated Collaborative approach for FM – Sydney Opera House

10.1   INTRODUCTION

The Sydney Opera House, the Australian Government, the CRC Construction Innovation, the Facility Management Association of Australia (FMA), and industry participants have a unique opportunity to support the Sydney Opera House as a Facility Management Exemplar Project (Facilities Management Action Agenda, 2005) that showcases innovative methods for improving FM performance and efficiency.

Benchmarking, procurement, and digital modelling for FM are three main study issues in the Sydney Opera House FM Exemplar Project. While each of these issues represents an important area of research, the research's purpose is to connect them all to create an integrated Facilities Management framework.

The research to date for the Sydney Opera House Facilities Management Exemplar Project is presented in this document.

- **Section 2** outlines a benchmarking framework for the SOH and the FM industry to identify best practices and set benchmarks of interest, which involves the development of key performance indicators and data gathering.

118

- **Section 3** examines procurement strategies based on the SOH examples, as well as the possibility of future collaboration between benchmarking and procurement via data exchange and key performance indicator references.

- **Section 4** discusses the development of digital modelling for facility management and proposals for an integrated platform for facility management that allows for data sharing and collaborative FM operations. A conclusion is provided in the concluding section.

10.2 REVIEW OF THE PAPER

The Sydney Opera House (SOH) is used as an instance case study in this research to illustrate an integrated collaborative approach to facilities management (FM). Benchmarking, Procurement, and Digital Modeling are all addressed in this strategy, which fosters collaboration between them. Its goal is to develop novel FM methods and concepts that will assist the Australian facilities management industry directly.

The Asset upkeep of the performing arts Center, iconic building, and facilities with similar functionalities is the subject of the Benchmarking theme. The SOH's organizational objectives are used to identify critical success elements in the functional domains of asset maintenance, and key performance indicators are produced. **The Procurement subject focuses on the procurement of maintenance services, particularly for outsourcing. Procurement strategies are reviewed, as well as a multi-criteria assessment strategy for decision support.**

Benchmarking and procurement should collaborate on the sharing of benchmarking data and the use of key performance indicators to support procurement strategy. The Digital Modelling subject explores the potential of state-of-the-art information technologies to enable a future integrated platform to support facility management collaborative activities and processes, as well as developing building information modelling for facilities management.

10.3 CONCLUSION

The Sydney Opera House FM Exemplar Project is a fantastic way to take advantage of the iconic character of the Sydney Opera House's international and national profile in order to find and create best practices in the FM sector. The customer, consultants, and service providers all contribute to this project in a variety of ways. The project's results will aid the Australian Government's Facilities Management Action Agenda.

The project's unique methodologies may be adopted at the strategic, management, and operational levels across the Facilities Management business, with demonstrable training and educational benefits leading to improved service delivery.

11. CASE STUDY-FAILURE

11.1   INTRODUCTION

According to Historical and Current Studies, the facility management sector is facing an ever-increasing issue that puts our public assets at danger. The call for additional money has gone global. Regrettably, the central and provincial governments shift responsibility for finding financing solutions to local authorities.

- **As a result, our public buildings** are suffering from chronic delayed maintenance, which increases the cost of ownership, increases liability exposure, and reduces the facility's projected usable life.

- **Furthermore, individuals who occupy the structures** are affected by the harmful effects of prolonged delayed maintenance. The tenants of the facilities have been found to have a reduction in overall performance in terms of the badly kept surroundings. This has an impact on all levels of schooling as well as governmental job performance.

- **The findings of a research on current practises** in public facilities management programmes are included in this article. The goal is to discover factors that contribute to or detract from well-run, efficient facilities departments.

- **Considering the nature of this business,** both objective and subjective aspects suffer because of unkempt environment. This has an impact on all levels of schooling, as well as employee performance in the public sector. The organisational structure and accompanying communication routes were objectively determined.

- **Through an interview procedure,** the lifetime of the facility purpose was examined and discussed critically. Responsibility, efficient communication, data-driven programme planning, resource allocation, verification of work completed, continual learning and development, and the use of technologies were among the 15 data points covered.

This Research also provided as a benchmark against which to compare the success of public facilities management practises in the past. The value of public assets has risen steadily throughout the years. During that period, technological advancements and innovation in operational practise provide new options for organisations to solve efficiency concerns that allow into a measure of quality. Given the ongoing demand for additional financing, it appears that difficulties persist despite the technologies.

The purpose of this research is to determine what those challenges are. Further research based on successful public facility management models reveals what techniques, if implemented, may help lower-performing programmes become more effective.

11.2 METHODOLOGY

The writer recently performed research with facility managers from the public sector, including towns, districts, institutions, and campuses. It discovered both **parallels and differences in terms of the issues** and solutions. Over the course of four months, a set of questionnaires were held with representatives from a wide range of public groups. Both organisational and operational questions were asked throughout the interviews. **There were fifteen issues discussed,** with the opportunity for further debate. Based on the subject, these conversations were carefully analysed for data and then collated within the team. For comparability, the objective data was also examined.

The focus of the research was to uncover the difficulties that hindered well-coordinated projects, but it also looked at what common features existed across the most efficient and least successful facility units.

11.3   REVIEW OF RESEARCH

Most of the managers voiced various levels of despondency, some of which bordered on defeat. A variety of obstacles were discovered in both the procedure and the sources. Priorities were treated as if they were a raging inferno, with reactionary measures frequently resulting in more costs and less effect.

- Many People were aware of their present **programmes' inefficiency and ineptness,** but they felt powerless in the face of an impossible challenge.

- Public facility managers highlighted a **variety of difficulties as a justification** for the present difficulty they have in managing and maintaining their assets in a recent survey performed by the author. **A lack of funds** was mentioned by 100 percent of respondents polled as the major impediment to efficiently and effectively managing their facilities.

- While this is correct, it is also a simple reason to **justify failure.** To put it another way, management was hampered by a **lack of finances, which prevented them from future objectives.** Following that first scream of despair, a consoling realisation that internal adjustments might be done to improve their facilities programmes emerged.

- A farewell question was offered to each of those questioned, as if they were king for a day.

All Obstacles were removed, giving them the freedom to make whatever modifications to their facilities programme that they believed would improve efficiency and effectiveness. From most to least common, the below were their top comments.

- **More Money** is needed.

- **Modify/improve** their current facility programme.

- **Conduct a thorough facility evaluation** in order to develop a data-driven strategy.

- **Increased workforce.**

From the Study Conducted, few challenges could be identified:

- **The General Shortage of Money and/or the insecurity of/** absence of a permanent funding source for facility upkeep was the major obstacle which was identified

- **All of the Other issues seem to stem** from a poor communication and good understanding amongst all parties involved, from finance to repair.

- **Misdirection of funds was another challenge.** According to the research, 78 percent of budget allocation choices were made above the facility management's role, with 22 percent including ruling board guidance.

11.4 SUMMARY AND CONCLUSION

In conclusion, the most prevalent issues mentioned by facility management in recent research can and have been demonstrated to be addressed using technology. The solution has been created to be simple to use. The requirement for a user-friendly solution was unquestionable, given the vast variety of current degrees of comfort within the facilities organisation.

70% of the facility managers polled indicated anxiety about their employees' incapacity to adapt to technological changes.

- **Furthermore, Because of the Ease of a Single Screen,** the problems of a complicated operation are no longer a worry. As a result, the transition to a technological solution may be done through the establishment of an employee training programme supported by on-line lessons in both video and PDF printed forms.

- **Past has shown that there is an ever-increasing difficulty in the administration of public infrastructure.** Property values have increased, expenditures have risen, and finance is in short supply and volatile. According to a recent survey, 100% of facility managers believe that finance is their biggest challenge.

- **They Recognised their lack of control over the situation and concluded that modifications in their operational procedures inside their programmes,** as well as enhanced usage of a data-driven strategy, would result in increased efficiency and, hence, efficacy.

- **The Only way to deal with a lack of revenue is to decrease costs.** There is no choice to decrease employees because, according to the survey, 64% of those interviewed believe they currently have a staffing shortage. As a result, the only option is to boost efficiency in order to get more done with less.

- **This Study proposes a method for substantially improving in-house facility management programmes.** Pathways for transparent communication based on shared data are established by combining user-friendly technologies.

- **There Must be quick and demonstrable beneficial benefits if the stated needs of effective communication and a data-driven programme are met.** These effects include increased worker productivity and a higher degree of clarity in the communication chain, resulting in fewer misunderstanding and erroneous choices.

- **Asset Maintenance will shift to a 70-80 percent proactive approach with 20-30 percent reactive labour,** as is the industry standard. Additionally, the beneficial influence on building tenants will increase their performance, contributing to overall improvements in the public facilities sector.

CHAPTER 12

12. CONCLUSION

- **Facilities Management** is a discipline that is always evolving since facilities are constantly changing. Facilities management best practices must adapt at the same time as the two grow together.

- **Facilities Management Methods** are increasingly focusing on leveraging data and analytics to improve decision-making as modern workplaces become more digitally connected. As a result, a more comprehensive, and personalized approach to managing buildings and the systems that govern them has emerged.

- **Learning Modern best practices** and applying them into everyday activities will help both new facilities managers and seasoned professionals. There are seven top facilities management best practices that you should implement at work.

12.1 CENTRALIZE FACILITY MANAGEMENT THROUGH SOFTWARE

The bane of proactive facilities management has long been siloed data. In one basket, there's real estate; in another, there's building maintenance; and yet another, there's space usage. Today, the situation is the opposite. FMs can gain a better understanding of how different sections of their facilities interact and what broad trends are prevalent by using holistic data and analytics.

In a conventional facilities management organization, breaking down silos requires technology that provides a top-down view:

- **Integrated Workplace Management System (IWMS)**

- **Computer Aided Facilities Management (CAFM)**

- **Computerized Maintenance Management System (CMMS)**

- **Enterprise Asset Management (EAM)**

12.2 STAY ABREAST OF TECHNOLOGY AND THE OFFICE IOT

Workplaces are becoming more intelligent. New technologies are constantly being developed, new iterations of current technologies are being released on a regular basis, and updates are being released to improve legacy equipment. It is the responsibility of a facility manager to keep up with technological changes.

Facility managers are looking for methods to improve their workplaces by incorporating Internet of Things (IoT) technology. How may technology assist you in doing your job more effectively? How can new choices complement or replace your existing systems? What difficulties will the Internet of Things address in facilities? The more you know about technology, the more likely you are to profit from the office IoT.

12.3 COLLECT AS MUCH INFORMATION AS POSSIBLE

Data and Analytics are at the heart of many of today's greatest facilities management approaches. Data from IoT devices empowers facility managers to make better decisions about the workplace and how to care for their buildings. This begins with identifying problems and locating data streams that have solutions. The first step in hypothesizing solutions is to quantify as much of the workplace as feasible.

12.4   RECOGNIZE AND CAPITALIZE ON TRENDS

- **Data Collection** is a crucial best practice but learning to analyses and use that data is just as critical. Data interpretation will not only tell you on the basic workings of your facilities, but it will also validate (or ify) your facility management improvement ideas.

- **Every Choice should be data-driven in the age of office IoT** and strong workplace management software. One of the most crucial best practices to master is recognizing and capitalizing on trends through data gathering and interpretation.

12.5   AUTOMATE FACILITIES PROCESSES

- **A Key Component of efficient facilities management** is streamlining operations. Automation takes it a step further, enhancing workplace structure in terms of both cost and quality.

- **Lights that are controlled by software save money on electricity.** Data collection that is automated aids decision-making. Support ticketing that is automated speeds up facility maintenance. The list might go on forever. Automation produces workplaces that are helpful and adaptable to both employees and the company.

12.6 MAKE BUDGETING A PRIORITY

- **As Facilities Management** becomes more closely aligned with reducing corporate expenses, proper budgeting becomes increasingly important.

- **Facilities Managers can budget more effectively** with the help of workplace data and analytics.

- **Recognizing cost-cutting opportunities,** avoiding unnecessary expenses, and properly budgeting for impending expenses all contribute to a company's financial health.

12.7 CUSTOMIZE MANAGEMENT TO YOUR FACILITIES

There is no one-size-fits-all approach to facilities management, as seen by the growth of customized best practices. There shouldn't be in an era when workplaces are becoming more complex.

Following best practices involves satisfying your workplace's demands in a way that positively mold and adds to the company.

REFERENCES

1. Nor, N. A. M., Mohammed, A. H. & Alias, B., 2014. Facility Management History and Evolution. *INTERNATIONAL JOURNAL OF FACILITY MANAGEMENT,* 5(1), pp. 1-21.

2. Alexander, K., 1994. A Strategy for Facilities. *MCB University Press,* 12(11), pp. 6-10.

3. Kima, K. et al., 2017. Integration of ifc objects and facility management work information using Semantic web. *Elseveir,* 1(1), pp. 173-187.

4. PAŠEK, J. & SOJKOVÁ, V., 2018. FACILITY MANAGEMENT OF SMART BUILDINGS. *Int. Rev. Appl. Sci. Eng,* 2(9), pp. 181 - 187.

5. Wahab, M. A. & Kamaruzzaman, S.-N., 2017. A Facility Management Strategies. *elsevier,* 1(1), pp. 1-14.

6. Lemaire, X. (2008) 'Sustainable Energy Regulation and Policy-Making for Africa', *Management*

7. www.environmentalleader.com

8. limblecmms.com

9. www.highspeedtraining.co.uk

10. https://www.highspeedtraining.co.uk/

11. www.iofficecorp.com

12. www.mordorintelligence.com

13. www.prnewswire.com

14. https://www.mordorintelligence.com/industry-reports/india-facility-management-market.

15. Indian Facilities Management Market: Growth Opportunities and Challenges Ahead

16. https://spaceiq.com/blog/facilities-management-best-practices/